SERGIO LEONE

Oreste De Fornari

SERGIO LEONE

The Great Italian Dream of Legendary America

GREMESE

TO MICHELA

Acknowledgements

Most of the photos in this book are by Angelo Novi, the set photographer for almost all of Leone's movies (he also played the part of a friar in *The Good, the Bad and the Ugly*). They were printed by Salvatore Casale and Bruno Bruni. The photos for *A Fistful of Dollars* are by Enrico Appetito, set photographer for that film, and those for the *The Colossus of Rhodes* were provided by André Chevailler of the Cinémathèque Suisse (Lausanne). Others were contributed by Mario Calderale from the magazine *Segno Cinema* and still others were courtesy of the private collections of Franco Castelnovi, Mario Natale, and Cristina Torelli of L'Officina Film Club of Rome.
I am also indebted for filmographies, data, bibliographies, details, authorizations, and other vital assistance to Claudio Mancini, Emma Ferrini, Claver Salizzato, Massimo Marchelli, Giorgio Navarro, Angelo Humouda, Anna Guedy, Marco Giusti and Aldo Tassone. My special thanks, finally, to Antonietta Pizzorno and Luc Moullet for their precious help.

Author's Note

The Italian edition of this book on Sergio Leone originally appeared in Italy in 1984 (Ubulibri editions) and in an abridged edition in 1977 (Moizzi editions). This English version coincides with a renewed interest (not only of critics) in the work of the Roman film director who died in 1989. The Spoleto '95 and Venice '96 festivals respectively presented restored editions (edited by Claver Salizzato) of *Once Upon a Time in the West* and *Duck! You Sucker*. A new edition of *Once Upon a Time in America* is being prepared which restores thirty-one minutes of footage that were sacrificed in the final version. These are privileges normally only reserved for the most illustrious members of cinema's hall of fame. Thirty years ago it would have been difficult to foresee that Leone would be studied in the universities and recognized as a great master even by American directors (Carpenter, Scorsese...). His movies, based on a reworking of popular myths that belong to our childhood, have always inspired in me a certain feeling of complicity as well as admiration.
And this has given rise to the present volume, more like an album, an unsuspecting mirror of the Leone style, that groups together: film reviews, a stylistic section, photographs, the director's own statements, testimonies of those who worked with him as well as detailed outlines of his films preceding each of my essays in the chapter, "Films." Of course, in the past, when it was not always easy to see films again and again, outlines and treatments were often precious study tools. I hope that now, in the age of video, they will still be found useful for specific purposes. Indeed, now the possibility of simply inserting a video-cassette when we want to view a few sequences has made us all like Italian opera habitués who drop by the theater only to listen to an aria or two. Thus the need for the libretto, that is, in our case the story outline.

Originally published in Italian as Tutti i film di Sergio Leone
© Ubulibri - Rome

On the cover:
Sergio Leone, photo by Angelo Novi

Translated from the Italian by:
Charles Nopar

Photocomposition and photolithography
Graffiti - Rome

Printed and bound by:
Tipolitografia Petruzzi Corrado & Co.
Città di Castello (Italy)

© 1997 Gremese International s.r.l.
P.O. Box 14335
00149 Rome

ISBN 88-7301-094-6

PHOTO CREDITS

Angelo Novi: pp. 8, 18, 19, 23 (above), 24, 57, 59, 62, 63, 64, 65, 66, 67, 68, 70, 72, 74-75, 76, 77, 78, 79 (right), 80, 81, 84, 87, 88, 89, 90, 92, 93, 94, 97, 98, 99, 100, 102, 103, 104, 105, 106, 107, 108, 109, 110, 111, 112, 113, 114-115, 116, 117, 121, 122 (above), 125, 128 (left), 130, 134, 138, 140, 144 (below), 146, 151, 155, 157, 160, 162.
Mario Natale collection: pp. 6, 12, 14, 21, 22, 25, 96, 101, 118, 120, 126-127, 132, 137, 142, 144 (above), 148-149, 161.
Enrico Appetito: pp. 15, 34, 36, 38, 39, 40, 42, 43, 44, 45, 122 (below).
Franco Castelnovi collection: pp. 46, 49 (above left), 50-51, 54, 55, 56, 123.
Cinémathèque Suisse archive: pp. 28, 30, 32, 33.
Cristian Torelli collection: pp. 17, 128 (right).
Segno Cinema archive: pp. 31, 49, (below and right), 61, 79 (left), 83.
Sergio Leone collection: pp. 23 (below), 53.

CONTENTS

Who Betrayed the Italian Cinema?

In Italy there are two kinds of cinema worthy of interest: on the one hand there is the auteur cinema, that of Rossellini, Visconti, Antonioni, Fellini, Pasolini and Bertolucci which, though much applauded by the critics, was for a long time ignored by the public; and on the other hand there is a kind of cinema based on the conventions of genres, such as that of Cottafavi, Bava, Matarazzo, and Jacopetti, despised by the Italian critics but which attracts crowds. Within this genre-type of moviemaking Sergio Leone beats all the records for provocation. At the very moment when the Italian cinema was fighting the invasion of American films with all the means at its command, Leone made almost exclusively Westerns, all set in America and shot in American English.

Whereas the quality of an Italian movie is often judged by its quota of neorealism, Leone makes fun of reality and is interested only in the past, never in the present. The cinema of social commitment dictates the rules of the game, yet Leone never takes sides (*Duck! You Sucker*). Leone is the traitor of the Italian cinema par excellence. And yet – as De Fornari's book well shows – these two kinds of moviemaking have solid bonds between them: Mario Monicelli and Dino Risi suddenly switch from the second type to the first, just as De Sica returned at the end of his career to making genre movies. Bertolucci collaborates in writing the script for a film of Leone's; Pasolini acts in a Western and casts the dubious comedians, Franco Franchi and Ciccio Ingrassia, in one of his pictures; Leone works as an assistant and an extra in *The Bicycle Thief* while Cottafavi goes from melodramas and historical costume movies to adaptations of Conrad and the Greek classics.

And nevertheless these genre films often turn out to be even more personal and artistic than the films of auteur cinema which nowadays are much too often reduced to a kind of left-wing reminiscence or fanciful flight of the aesthete (Scola, Brusati, Pontecorvo, Cavani, Bolognini, Petri, Vancini, Maselli, Lizzani, Zeffirelli, etc.).

With his aggressive editing, Leone is the principal heir of Eisenstein. He reaches the levels of the most modern moviemaking structured upon the film's length. Like Rivette, Leone cannot make a successful movie if he does not stretch it out to at least two and a quarter hours. His first pictures were too short, and only with *The Good, the Bad and the Ugly* was Sergio Leone able to really be himself. There is a new concept of time in him which contains the essence of his genius and is based on extension.

Above and beyond the differences that the size of the audiences or hasty labelling might seem to underline, Marguerite Duras comes to mind. But whereas in Duras the extension of time expresses everyday reality, material or moral, in Leone it infiltrates genres – action films, Westerns – where speed reigns supreme. Another provocation, more provocative than Duras. Speed exists in Leone's work, excessive, preposterous speed: in the wink of an eye several gun-loads of bullets are fired, but only after an unlikely ceremonial, five minutes long, articulated by countless close-ups contrary to narrative logic, where no action takes place. This rhythm is contradictory, as is the constant accumulation of vulgar with majestic elements. We are not far from Menotti and his opera of the dismal. It is a rare example of avant-garde moviemaking understood and adored by a vast public.

Admirable and precarious work, like that of Syberberg or Jancso, it relies upon the discovery of new formal principles (I almost wrote new formulas) whose interest may wane very quickly, and this helps us understand Leone's "fear of filming."

Luc Moullet (1983)

James Woods and Robert De Niro in Once Upon a Time in America.

When the Audience Applauded

There is the story of that winter afternoon in 1966 when Sergio Leone, in his office, sees three menacing types burst in, demanding in Roman dialect: "*Perfessor* – we seen the movie twenny times, we bet our shirts an' ya gotta tell us – was she the daughter or the sister?"

Their curiosity regarded Leone's most recent movie *For a Few Dollars More*, and in particular the relationship between Lee Van Cleef and the girl who was raped in the flashback scene, whose portrait he keeps in his pocket watch, and whom he avenges by killing her assailant. Despite an explanatory exchange of remarks (Eastwood: "There's a family resemblance in this picture." Van Cleef: "It can happen between brother and sister sometimes."), the three Romans hadn't gotten it. Perhaps the lines were drowned out by cries or applause – that was something that often happened during Westerns, especially when they were directed by Leone. It is well known that the popular cinema in Italy had very brief seasons of success. The Western boom went the way of the horror film, the mythology film, the opera film, etc. Not exactly genres, just barely veins.

The genre is an industrial product which requires a steady flow of investment. The vein belongs more to a robber economy: intensively exploited, it is soon exhausted. Furthermore, a vein is aimed at a circumscribed audience, at times only regional, as in the case of the Neapolitan movies of the fifties. Only the Italian-style comedy, an average product par excellence, has seemed able to escape this precarious situation: regular teams of directors and writers, recurring characters and actors, the constant popularity among a heterogeneous audience.

Leone's movies also enjoyed the very same success as this type of comedy, in both the big movie houses and the neighborhood dives. Unlike Dino Risi or Luigi Comencini, Leone does not try to tone down the more sophisticated or vulgar elements, but rather intensifies them: there are farce-like lines that stand next to those of an almost hermetic refinement. Faced with certain prolonged silences (Lee Van Cleef entering the Mexican farm in *The Good, the Bad and the Ugly*), the exasperated audience would be known to cry out, "When is he gonna make up his mind to talk!" – something that otherwise would only happen sometimes in the films of Antonioni. But these were more symptoms of impatience than of discontent. On the other hand, certain critics literally detested Leone. They called him a "mannerist" which in those austere days was to be considered tantamount to an insult. Now thirty years later, mannerism is in vogue and the borderlines between cultivated and popular genres have finally been abolished. Leone is now considered a classic, in a way. One speaks of *Once Upon a Time in the West* as a metawestern, a deconstructionist western, as the cinema reflecting upon itself. Umberto Eco compared Leone's "godless nostalgia" for the West to that of Ariosto's for the Middle Ages.

But such high-flying phrases are not very suitable to his work. One risks forgetting that the public once practically wrecked movie theaters to see his films, that moralists accused Leone of being an apologist for violence, and that some film buffs learned his dialogues by heart. It even reached the point where the music of *Once Upon a Time in the West* was played at weddings in place of Mendelssohn's *Wedding March*.

Oreste De Fornari

LEONE ON LEONE

"I began as assistant to De Sica, Camerini, Soldati, Gallone, Bonnard..." Aldo Fabrizi and Sergio Leone on the set of Hanno rubato un tram *directed by Mario Bonnard.*

The Beginnings

"My father, Roberto Roberti, began his acting career in 1904 with Eleonora Duse. In 1908 he started directing and shot about ninety films in all, quite a few of them with the actress Francesca Bertini. *Contessa Sara* ran for nine months in a Rome movie house. I remember seeing a photo showing the mounted police controlling the crowds at the entrance. It was he who discovered the actor to play Maciste, Bartolomeo Pagano. Pagano was working as a stevedore at the port of Genoa, and my father presented him to Pastrone. He is also the director of a very fine version of *Fra Diavolo* [Friar Devil] with Gustavo Sereni and Lido Manetti, who was killed in Hollywood under mysterious circumstances – apparently by the Mafia because he was threatening to take the place of Rudolph Valentino. When Ernst Lubitsch went to Hollywood, my father was called to replace him as the director of Pola Negri. But my mother was against it and so it is by pure chance that I wasn't born in Germany.

"My father was one of the first to enroll in the Fascist Party. He paid his first dues and after ten days they came to tell him he had to pay them again because the secretary had run off with the cash box. From that moment he became an anti-Fascist. He was saved from internment thanks to an old school chum, Roberto Forges Davanzati, who had become a minister, but for a long time was not able to shoot a film. When we went out on Sundays to the Café Aragno we were followed at a distance by two policemen. During that long period of inactivity my father was reduced to misery. This ostracism ended in 1942 thanks to an influential member of the Regime and my father was able to shoot *La bocca sulla strada* [Mouth on the street] in Naples with Armando Falconi. The following year I was his assistant director for *I fuochi di San Martino* [Fires of San Martino] with Aldo Silvani. That was his last film. Then he gave up moviemaking and retired to Torella dei Lombardi between Avellino and Naples where he had been born and there he died soon after.

"I never had the chance to learn from him. I began as an assistant to Vittorio De Sica, Mario Camerini, Mario Soldati, Carmine Galloni, and Mario Bonnard... I was technical director for an episode of *Questa è la vita* [This is life] (from Pirandello's story *La marsina stretta*) [The tight tailcoat] interpreted by Aldo Fabrizi." (ODF '83)

"I also worked with the Americans: Mervyn Le Roy's *Quo Vadis?* in 1951, *Helen of Troy* with Wise in 1958 (I was in Walsh's second unit which had filmed all the battle and the landing, then I was transferred to the first unit with Wise, who hadn't wanted to do this film), and Zinnemann's *The Nun's Story* in 1959. But, above all, *Ben Hur* with Wyler again in 1959.

"Wyler had signed a contract that stipulated he would in no way concern himself with the chariot race which would be entirely in the hands of the second unit. He would see a projection of the result and if it did not please him it would be shot all over again until he was satisfied.

"I was assistant director in the second unit directed by Andrew Marton. We had two months for preparing the horses and more than three for the shooting.

"I had to see Fred Niblo's version of *Ben Hur* an awful lot of times because they showed it every night and the troupe was obliged to attend the projection." (GB '69)

"This is the best way to learn. I always tell those who ask to be a voluntary assistant: 'You should come and watch me shoot a film and then escape, especially if you love my movies, because you risk becoming an imitator as happened with Zeffirelli under Visconti. It's better to be an assistant to three or four directors whom you esteem and then some less excellent directors in order to make comparisons and decide what you would do in their place.' As an assistant director I made some films where I earned more than the director did because he needed me for the technical side. I was the one to tell him where to place the camera.

"When I was twenty-five I received a proposal to direct some minor Italian films, but I refused because I wanted to delay my directing debut. I was afraid of ruining my career and involving the producer in an economic disaster. I believe that Loy, Petri, and Bolognini acted similarly. In those days we had more sense of responsibility.

"I made The Colosssus of Rhodes *in 1960 to pay for my honeymoon
trip to Spain." Sergio Leone on the set of the film.*

"*Last Days of Pompeii* was begun by Bonnard who then abandoned it to make *Gastone,* and I, who was with the second unit, went over to the first and chose Corbucci (whom at the time no one wanted) to direct the second unit and Duccio Tessari as assistant director.

"At first the hero was supposed to be a kind of Scarlet Pimpernel or James Bond – intelligent, witty. Then when we got to Spain, the producers (Procusa, an Opus Dei company) told us they had managed to sign up Steve Reeves. So in ten days we had to rewrite the script to suit this muscular actor. But *The Colossus of Rhodes,* where the hero is a playboy, is more to my taste." (ODF '83)

"I have no nostalgia for mythological subjects. I made *The Colossus of Rhodes* in 1960 for bread and butter, to pay for my honeymoon trip to Spain. Forced into a choice I said, 'I want to try making a film with the same ingredients but in an ironic vein.' I had been remotely inspired, actually, by a film of Hitchcock's, *North by Northwest:* a person takes a trip to an accursed island for a rest, and in spite of himself he becomes involved in all kinds of things that push him to take action. Certainly it was not the kind of thing I really liked. I do not even like *Spartacus,* however well made it was. The only interesting thing of the kind I have seen was an English television series on domestic life in ancient Rome.

"*The Colossus of Rhodes* enjoyed a lot of success, so much success that I was forced to refuse six Maciste films a day. When they offered me two of these movies I had 200,000 lire [about 200 dollars] in my bank account. I put off signing until the next day. Carla, my wife, said: 'If you really don't feel like it, refuse. Something else will turn up.' What turned up was a film script and then Robert Aldrich who asked me to be his assistant in *Sodom and Gomorrah.* It was a big disappointment because I had deeply admired the latest things Aldrich had made, *Attack!* and *The Big Knife,* but when I found myself faced with reality it was all different. Then I left, deserted the set, explaining that I didn't want to help bury an Italian producer. I sent a good letter to Lombardo, saying: 'Instead of fishing around in the South Seas, come back at once with a machine gun and when you land at Marrakesh, don't worry too much but just shoot, whomever you hit it will be okay, since this is a criminal organization: they're murdering you.' And in fact, the movie had those misadventures which, together with the failure of *The Leopard,* led to the bankruptcy of Titanus." (ODF '88)

A Fistful of Dollars

"Italy was in the midst of a movie-industry crisis. Remember the bankruptcy of Titanus. And so the films taken from Karl May's books, a kind of German equivalent of our Emilio Salgari were successful. On the European level it was thought that to reduce financial risks it would be a good idea to make Westerns. In that case, in fact, Spanish and German producers would be willing to join in. But one thing I must make clear: many people think I am the father of the Italian Western. It's not true. Before me twenty-five Westerns had been made.

"When I finished *A Fistful of Dollars,* a Roman movie-house owner, with no less than fifty theaters, did not even want to come and see the film because it had been deemed by then that the Western in Italy was totally finished.

"The other Italian Westerns had already been released and the critics had not even noticed. For three years they had

Clint Eastwood during the filming of **Il magnifico straniero,** *the first title of* **A Fistful of Dollars.**

already been doing re-runs of them on the neighborhood circuits and no one had noticed because they were all presented with false names and it was thought that they were minor films, American television releases, and no one guessed for a minute that they were made by Italian and Spanish directors; and so let's say that *A Fistful of Dollars* was the twenty-sixth Italian Western.

"Ten years ago, when I began to shoot films, coming from a neo-realist school I could not imagine that four years later I would make my debut with such a thing as a Western. One day I noticed that the genre was languishing, I had seen some of the recent American productions that were pretty stale, and I thought: 'Why should such a noble kind of cinema have to die?' For, in a Western you can treat such wide-ranging and important themes in such a way as to make the genre truly noble.

"After seeing *Yojimbo* I thought of bringing back home the American novel on which Kurosawa had based his movie and I dedicated myself with great passion but little means to working on the film. The producers did not realize that a film was in the making that would give a new special direction to movie-making and so I was kind of the little brother. In fact, the same producers were making another movie at the same time, Mario Caiano's *Le pistole non discutono* [Guns don't talk], which was full of commonplaces, the final charge, etc., etc., and they had given all of the money to him. For example, one American actor alone, Rod Cameron, cost as much as my whole cast put together because they thought it was an A-movie whereas *A Fistful of Dollars* was thought to be kind of a salvage job.

"When I spoke with these gentlemen, to be precise with a certain so-called producer Giorgio Papi, I told him that I wanted Gian Maria Volonté as the hero, and he said: 'You're nuts, Leone, go away and play, have your fun, I don't even want to see the film – anyway we're ahead of the game to start with.' For them it was just a business deal and that was very much to my advantage because I had complete autonomy and there was no interference from the producers. So I went off to Spain and did my seven weeks of shooting and what came out of it was *A Fistful of Dollars*." (FF '71)

"I was the first to make Westerns without women. I anguished for six long months after having finished *A Fistful of Dollars* (which furthermore had cost the Italian producer only 30 million lire) because somebody had read the treatment and mistaken it for a comedy, while someone else asked how you

could dream of making a film without women. A big Florence movie-house owner who today doesn't have the courage to face me said: 'My dear Leone, you have made a film which can never be successful because it is absurd that the only woman in it is an extra.' And I replied that I was intentionally shooting a movie without women, that it was all calculated in advance. I had seen John Sturges' excellent *Gunfight at the O.K. Corral* (which was later badly remade) and had asked myself what Rhonda Fleming was doing in it. She stopped the rhythm of the movie. If during the editing they had cut her part it would have been a more serious movie. Maybe her part was inserted for atavistic reasons.

The Western was the first kind of film ever to be made, and so women were considered indispensable for the female public, but it was demonstrated that women liked *A Fistful of Dollars* just because there were no women in it... And maybe they even thought: 'That hero is the way he is because he never met *me!*'" (MM '78)

"I wanted Lavagnino, who had composed the music for *The Colossus of Rhodes*, to write the score. At the Jolly they had spoken to me of Ennio Morricone and showed me *Duello nel Texas* [Showdown in Texas] which seemed horrible to me; the music sounded like a poor man's Tiomkin. The producer insisted on my meeting Morricone. I went to his house and he recognized me at once. We had been classmates in fifth grade at Saint Juan Baptiste de la Salle, with the Piarist Brothers where I also did my high school studies. He had me listen to a piece that the producers had rejected and which I was later to use in the finale of the film. Afterwards we listened to a record of something he had written for an American baritone which immediately impressed me. I asked him to keep the basic musical elements. We had the principal motif, only the singer was lacking. I proposed having someone whistle it and thus the firm Alessandroni and Company was born which later worked on many Westerns." (ODF '83)

For a Few Dollars More

"The bounty hunter was an ambiguous figure. In the West he was called "the undertaker." He fascinated me because he represented the way of life in this country: the need to kill in order to survive...

"This reminds me of an anecdote about Wyatt Earp. Just after being named sheriff of a small town he goes out looking for a card sharp. To demonstrate his power, he provokes him, challenges him to a showdown, and kills him. At that very moment he hears footsteps behind him, turns and shoots his assistant between the eyes, killing him. That is what the period was like and the bounty hunter was a typical figure." (GB '69)

"I wanted Lee Marvin for the part of Mortimer. I left Rome on a Friday and was supposed to start shooting with him on Monday at Cinecittà. Just before leaving I got a phone call from Marvin's agent: the contract had fallen through because Marvin had signed for *Cat Ballou*. I was desperate. I left for Los Angeles with the production director Ottavio Oppo. I remembered Lee Van Cleef in *Bravados* and in *High Noon* where he was called 'machine gun' for the way he used pistols. I remembered him as being a bit like a Roman barber, all dark and curly-haired, and that worried me.

"But Lee Van Cleef seemed to have disappeared. They told me he had stopped working. He had gone to dry out in a clinic for alcoholics and had ended up with his car in a Los Angeles canyon. He was covered with silver plates and nails. To earn a living he had taken up painting pictures. He painted like a young lady, all landscapes and seascapes...

"When I found him in a hotel foyer he was wearing a dirty trench coat that reached down to his feet and cowboy boots. His salt-and-pepper hair had a brush cut. He looked like an eagle, he looked like Van Gogh.

"I said to Ottavio Oppo: 'He is so right for the part that I don't even want to talk to him, because if I talk to him maybe I won't find him intelligent and I will make a big mistake. Go and sign him up at once.' Instead he is anything but stupid, he is a Dutch Jew and he calls himself Van Cleef like the jewelers.

"He said he had to deliver a picture. They had given him fifty dollars and he had to go collect another hundred and fifty. He thought we wanted to have him shoot two or three scenes. When he realized he would be the co-lead in the movie he almost fainted. He began sharing the $5,000 advance with his agent as if he had hit a gold mine.

"He was very grateful to me, and two years later when we were doing the dubbing in New York, he invited me to a marvelous Chinese restaurant with his wife and ex-nurse he had met in the hospital (he needed someone to keep him under control). I said to her: 'What a lovely fur.' She smiled at me: 'We owe it to you. Two years ago we were having trouble paying the light bill.' (ODF '83)

The Good, the Bad and the Ugly

"I began this film just like the two preceding ones, with three characters and a treasure hunt. But what interested me was, on the one hand the demystification of words, and, on the other, the absurdity of war. What do good, bad and ugly mean? We are all a little good, a little bad, and a little ugly. And there are people who seem bad, but when you get to know them they aren't really...

"To my mind, civil war is useless, stupid, there are no just causes. The key line of the film is the comment made by a character about the battle on the bridge: 'I have never seen so many imbeciles die, and so pointlessly.' I was inspired by photographs of Union and Confederate prison camps (at Andersonville, for example, 250,000 prisoners died) for the movie's Union prison camp where the cries of the tortured prisoners are drowned out by the orchestra. Of course I also had in mind the Nazi concentration camps and the orchestras

Eli Wallach on the set of The Good, the Bad and the Ugly.

Sergio Leone on the set of The Good, the Bad and the Ugly.

of Jews... It is a little in the spirit of one of the greatest films I have ever seen, *Monsieur Verdoux*... That doesn't keep the movie from being able to make you laugh. There is a picaresque spirit in these tragic situations. The picaresque genre is an exclusively Spanish literary tradition that has some equivalents even in Italy in works like *Fra Diavolo*. In the picaresque as in the *commedia dell'arte* there are no entirely good or bad characters.

Nevertheless in *The Good, the Bad and the Ugly* it was impossible to let the worst of the three survive, who was played by a truly vicious Lee Van Cleef..." (GB '69)

"I wanted Eli Wallach because of a gesture he makes in *How the West Was Won* when he gets off the train and talks to George Peppard. He sees a child, Peppard's son, and suddenly turns and shoots him with a finger making a raspberry. That made me realize he was a comic actor of the Chaplin school, a Neapolitan Jew; you could ask him to do anything. In fact we had a very good time working together. He always wanted me to show him the movements he was to make, but just for a laugh." (ODF '83)

Once Upon a Time in the West

"In all my films one of the dominant themes, as you can see, is male friendship, which may be the only sentiment that is still left. And the Western for me is the virility of the individual, and therefore also vengeance. In *Once Upon a Time in the West* vengeance exists, it is precise, it is Bronson's obsession. But after he obtains it he says: 'I am finished. I don't know where to go. My life ends here.' He has lost his interest in life. Why do I begin with the great boredom of the three killers? Why, because killers are bored when not playing at the game of life and death! In fact the first of them duels with a fly, the second with a drop of water, the third with his hands – until the man to be killed shows up and then the fly is eliminated while the other one 'drinks this rusty water like a holy chalice' and thus they take care of the next guy and make an end of it, and die, because it is right and logical that they should die.

"So vengeance is part of life. In *For a Few Dollars More* there is one character who, having gotten his revenge, gives up all his work saying: 'Kid, the West is all yours. I've done my job and maybe I'll do like Cincinnatus and go back to tilling my fields.'" (MM '78)

"If I use so many close-ups in my movies (while in American Westerns the characters are more or less set against the landscape) its because I give so much importance to the eyes. That is where you can read everything: courage, threat, fear, uncertainty, death, etc. When Fonda has killed his enemies in the street with the help of Bronson on the balcony and he looks up at him, his whole character, his whole problem is in that look and also a presentiment of his end, because all that counts for him now is to understand what Bronson wants. I constructed the film like a jig-saw puzzle, like a mosaic where if you move one piece it ruins everything. Because none of the characters talks about himself, it is always someone else who judges him, reads him... You will have noticed that I always set the finales of my films inside a circle: that is where Lee kills Volonté, where Clint, Eli and Lee duel, where Bronson kills Fonda. It is the arena of life, the moment of truth, and that is

Upper photo: *Sergio Leone*
Lower photo: *Sergio Leone with Claudia Cardinale during the shooting of* Once Upon a Time in the West.

why I framed the shot to take in the landscape behind Bronson and Fonda." (GB '69)

"Fonda had my three films shown to him one after the other in Los Angeles, and when he came out he said: 'Where's the contract?'

"He showed up on the set with sideburns, a beard and dark contact lenses. I didn't say anything to him, but I didn't shoot his scenes, and day after day I removed one bit at a time: first the sideburns, then the beard, the moustache and finally the contact lenses. When he saw that I had focused the camera at the nape of his neck for his first appearance, he exclaimed: 'Jesus Christ, now I understand.' I wanted the public to recognize in this villain the same Fonda who had played all the good American presidents. And anyway, it's the truth. The vice presidents of the companies I have dealt with have all had baby-blue eyes and honest faces and what sons of bitches they were! Furthermore he's no saint himself. He has had five wives. The last one fell out the window while trying to murder him. He stepped over her and went to act his part in *Mr. Roberts* as if nothing had happened.

"I had some problems with the love scenes, but Claudia helped a lot. She behaved as if she had a man of twenty-five on top of her instead of sixty-five. And he played the scene with his usual classic sobriety." (ODF '83)

"Bronson was just the actor I wanted. By the time I went to America looking for him I was very well known and so I had a mob of agents offering me all the biggest names. And when I asked for Charlie Bronson they asked astonished: 'Who?' The rumor even began circulating that I was mad. And yet Bronson was most important for me because that face of his could stop a train. He was the executioner who even if you went to Greenland would follow you there and find you. He was exactly the archetype that I was seeking and whom I found in him alone. As an actor he is good, as American actors are, the ones who study themselves in a mirror controlling almost every facial muscle, who know everything.

"My first films were a bit tatty, partly because of the meager funds that I had available. Some of the costumes I would like to redo, improve, bring up to the level of the last films. In *A Fistful of Dollars,* for example, there were some things that weren't right just because I couldn't go and rummage – as I did for the later films – in the Western Costume warehouses in Hollywood among Ford's and his friend's old things. Western Costume is a kind of Rinascente (an Italian department store, *Ed.*) of costumes which has been financed for at least forty years by the

major American studios who have 20% of the stock. All the costumes used by Paramount, Fox, Metro, Universal and Columbia end up in this immense building, from collars, to shoes, to cuffs... In short, everything that has been made, ends up there. Naturally when I went there they showed me all the very newest things, beautiful things, that I had already seen in television films. But I explained that I was an Italian director with a very limited budget, and was wondering if they didn't have any warehouse leftovers. And they told me that they had a lot of stuff in the basements, but that they were practically rags. The search was extremely easy just because the costumes were all piled up in a huge room and after a month of hunting there with my costume designer I found everything I wanted. Things turned up which were later used in a lot of other American movies. Beginning with movies like *Butch Cassidy* certain directors demanded only these kinds of costumes. For this reason the cost of renting them went up from five to a hundred dollars and nobody wanted the new costumes anymore...

"I brought over dust from Monument Valley because I wanted that kind of color. The interiors of *Once Upon a Time in the West* were clearly shot at Cinecittà, but I still demanded dust of that color (and not only because the interiors had to correspond to the exteriors). When Bronson and Fonda came on that set they were astonished at the atmosphere which was so totally different; the actors, psychologically, performed differently. To my mind, when Visconti is attacked for his fussiness it is a mistake.

"For me the music is fundamental, especially in a Western where the dialogue is purely aphoristic; the films could just as well be silent; one would understand all the same. The music serves to emphasize states of mind, facts and situations more than the dialogue itself does. In a word, for me the music functions as dialogue. I have an almost visceral relationship to Ennio Morricone. I throw as many adjectives at him as I need to, until he gets the idea. At least twelve or thirteen themes are composed for my films and rejected; not because they are ugly (on the contrary they may be the prettiest ones), but because they don't give me the right sensations. This, on the other hand, is what music means to me: on hearing Shostakovich's 7th, a film to make came into my head... Perhaps the fact that I sing so very off pitch is the reason why I am so musical inside." (MM '78)

"It's very easy working with Sergio. We understand each other in just one look, without saying a word." Claudia Cardinale and Sergio Leone during the filming of Once Upon a Time in the West.

Ford, Peckinpah, and Me

"Ford was an optimist; I am a pessimist. When Ford's characters open a window, what they see, in the end, is a horizon full of hope, while mine are always afraid of getting a bullet between the eyes when they open a window. So for me Ford's best movie was one of his last, *The Man Who Shot Liberty Valance,* where he rediscovered pessimism: he understood that he was wrong, that he had not been a good prophet, so he went back and told things the way they were.

"I love Ford very much, but I criticize him even while loving him. I criticize him the way one can criticize Capra, that Italian full of the lust for success. The doors of success open to him, he believes in that beautiful America and, naturally, he makes films of that epoch, tied to that period." (MM '78)

"Furthermore, in America a certain kind of optimistic rhetoric is obligatory, even Huston told me that. To put *A Fistful of Dollars* on TV they added a preamble where a stand-in for Clint, wearing a poncho like his, speaks to the warden of a prison who promises him a reward and maybe even his freedom, if he sets things straight in that village. They did this without saying a word to me about it, just for the sake of a moral.

"Peckinpah once said: 'Without Leone I wouldn't have been able to make my movies.' Kubrick too said the same thing concerning *A Clockwork Orange. A Fistful of Dollars* was a trail-blazing film, at least for the way in which it depicted violence. Of Peckinpah's films *Guns in the Afternoon* is one that I liked a lot. The later ones, like *Straw Dogs,* I liked less. One

feels how alcohol has ruined the idea, everything becomes deformed, excessive... That happens to many. Even Coppola's *Apocalypse Now* strikes me as not having been shot in a state of complete lucidness." (ODF '83)

"By now I think the Western is everyone's heritage. But one should not confuse the myth of the West with the historical reality of America in the last century. If it is true that Western films are inspired by that period, it is equally true that they shape them at will. I remember one movie: *The Culpepper Co.,* a film about the West which however did not capture the mythical quality that comes from the legend and, above all, from the Hollywood films. Rather it was based on a rigorous historical reconstruction. People wouldn't buy it. Why? Because they did not find in it what they were looking for: the fable. That is the point: the fable, the telling of fables; the myths do not belong to anyone but to everyone. And so the Western too belongs to everyone!" (LV '79)

"When I made Westerns I always had in mind the *pupi*, the Sicilian marionettes. I re-read all the plots that inspired the Sicilian bards' songs: there was a strange affinity between the *pupi* and my Western friends. There adventures were identical. Only the background was changed. There is very little room for invention..." (GL '76)

Duck! You Sucker

"This is a film that I was only supposed to have produced. But Peter Bogdanovich, with whom I began working, conceived the

During the shooting of Duck! You Sucker. *Sergio Leone with Irish revolutionaries (*above*) and with a Mexican policeman (*below*).*

subject in an old Hollywood style. Then the actors refused to work with my assistant. So I proposed it to Sam Peckinpah, but Steiger would only accept his part if I directed personally.

"At first I wanted to have a great difference in age between the two leads who were to have a father-son relationship but in reverse. I had thought of Malcolm McDowell for the part of Sean and Jason Robards for that of Juan.

"Three months before starting shooting, Steiger hired at his own expense a Mexican girl to learn the language. And during all the production, up to the post-synchronization phase, he continued to speak Spanish on and off the set. "Coburn had spent five weeks in Ireland to perfect his accent. They did these things on their own initiatives out of professional seriousness.

"The film is very precise when it comes to certain details such as the armored car (which was the first model the Germans sent to Mexico), the machine guns, the train, the pistols which are of Belgian, German or American manufacture, the motorcycle, the colonial hats. But I do not aim at historical accuracy; I prefer the spirit of the fable. I start out with a historical situation taken as a pretext, and with a genre such as the Western to go beyond them.

"The corpses in the grotto, the executions in the ditches, the flight of the governor on the train, correspond for me (and this the Italian public understands) to precise episodes of the fight against Fascism, above all the executions in the Fosse Ardeatine and Mussolini's flight. (The officer who tries to escape disguised as a civilian and is shot in the back is played by an engineer who is a double for Mussolini in his youth.)

"I go back to Chaplin for my model whose comedies did more for Socialism than any political leader ever did. The sequence in the bank, with Steiger who finds himself at the head of the liberated prisoners, is taken directly from *Modern Times*." (GB '72)

"I had some problems with the actors, mostly with Steiger, who, like a good professional, wanted to know right from the start *everything* he had to do. I had a hard time making it clear that I didn't know anything yet, that I would decide from day to day. He kept on insisting: 'I want the script!' One day I pointed to my head. For a moment I was afraid he would break it open in order to read the invisible script...

"Coburn is a great professional. When he saw Steiger roll his eyes with histrionic dramatics, he tried competing with him. I made him understand that the less he tried to imitate him the better it would be. Coburn is very intelligent and understood at once, so in the film his measured interpretation makes a splendid counterpoint to Steiger. But Steiger acted better than usual. Since he is good only when he is tired, I made him repeat the same scene as many as forty times. He got mad. They calmed him down by saying: 'Leone is like a kid at the puppet show. He enjoys seeing you act so much that he makes you repeat the scene.'" (GL '76)

"I have little faith in political movies, so just imagine how I feel about these here. One thing that always made me smile was that when I went to Germany (where my movies had a really brilliant success), no one asked me about Fellini or Visconti but about what Corbucci was doing, maintaining that his films were political. And this made me laugh until I cried.

"When *Soldier Blue* was released, everyone cried 'miracle' and thought it was a progressive Western. What a lot of nonsense! Like a good craftsman, Ralph Nelson had knocked together what an intelligent producer thought he could sell: 'let's shoot a kind of mea culpa because this is the moment for spitting on ourselves.' To mistake this for a political film is typical of the European mentality: our false intellectualizing.

"As far as 'intelligent' Westerns go, I have only seen one of Sollima's films, *The Big Gundown,* whose title was my suggestion: I got it from a musical theme of Morricone's. A very fine subject by Franco Solinas completely ruined by a banal and stupid movie. In short, I have a very bad opinion of these

movies. So much so that when they tell me 'you are the father of the Italian Western' I think: 'What a lot of sons of bitches...'" (MM '78)

"I don't like fake political films, the film as a political rally. I prefer certain indirect political movies such as Wilder's *Front Page* or Forman's *One Flew Over the Cuckoo's Nest* which hit the audience harder than party slogans could do. And then, you cannot be a Communist with a villa. At best you might be able to be a bit of an anarchist." (ODF '83)

Once Upon a Time in America

"The story of this film started way back in 1967. The late Giuseppe Colizzi, who before making his debut in a Western with *Blood River* did an apprenticeship with me for a year (helping to shoot and edit *The Good, the Bad and the Ugly*), told me about a novel, *The Hoods,* upon which the episode of the robbery at the casino in *Revenge at El Paso* was based. The novel struck me as a modest affair but full of curious details. In New York I contacted Harry Grey, an old Jew from Odessa, who had been a gangster, had been Frank Costello's right-hand man. In fact the novel makes mention of a certain Frank, and Max too

Above: *In* Duck! You Sucker, *the end of Mussolini (Biagio la Rocca) as seen by Leone.* **Opposite**: *Sergio Leone with Michelangelo Antonioni.*

was inspired by a real person. At 73 years of age they offered Grey another job, but his wife advised him against it and after two months, they saw him in handcuffs on TV. Grey had written the novel during the fifteen years he spent in Sing Sing (but if you ask me his wife, an elementary school teacher, really did the writing). Grey told me he had written it to contest the films he had seen about gangsters in Sing Sing, but what struck me about it was precisely its similarity to Hollywood films. Fantasy had won out over reality. But you could tell that the episodes about his adolescence were things he had really experienced.

"For Noodles' three ages I had resigned myself to using different actors (for example, Paul Newman and Tom Berenger, the kid from *Oltre la porta* [Beyond the door] who was identical to Newman) when the producer told me he had finally managed to sign De Niro whom I had had in mind from the start. It was as if they had told Collodi, 'use a real person for Pinocchio.' It was supposed to be more of a mythic film, more a fable, but De Niro's extreme sincerity introduced a more realistic note. It is probably a little different from my other movies where pulling the marionette's strings provided an extra thrill.

"It is also an intimate movie that follows the memories of one man. It is probably the first time ever that a film ends with a flashback, so that Noodles could have even dreamed his future under the influence of opium; it could all have been an imaginary adventure. For the rest, I have no right to investigate American history except by way of parable.

"For ten weeks we shot in Italy and for twenty abroad (Paris, Montreal, New York). I took my troupe of forty-five people with me to the States and also engaged an American troupe which, to tell the truth, was not of much use to me. But despite this we had problems with the unions and had to return to Italy earlier than we had planned. Among the scenes we couldn't shoot was the one with the opening titles.

"Noodles, fleeing from New York in 1933 on a rainy night asks a truck driver for a lift: 'Where are you heading?' 'Wherever you are.' We are in open country near a railroad crossing. A train coming from Detroit passes by transporting cars, hundreds of 1930 Fords. Noodles' eyes rest on the train's wheels. When he raises them the train has become a modern one transporting 1968 models. When all the cars have rolled past a completely changed landscape is revealed, the outskirts of a city with skyscrapers. Beyond the railroad crossing, sitting at the wheel of a car, there is De Niro thirty years older. The

"In America, all the actors are good, even the beginners." Sergio Leone with Darlanne Fleugel during the **shooting of Once Upon a Time in America.**

barrier crossing goes up and the title appears: *Once Upon a Time in America.*

"The first producer, Grimaldi, wanted to make it a two-part film as he had done for *1900,* but Milchan (of *The King of Comedy*) would not hear of it. I told him: 'We are lucky to have De Niro, let's stop and think it over for a moment, let's go over the script again, let's make a single movie, compressed'; but he made me understand that if we did not start at once we would never succeed in making the movie. So during the shooting I cut what I could even while realizing we would end up with a film as long as two." (ODF '83)

"My script did not call for that smile at the end. It is clear that having an actor like De Niro, I can end it that way. If I had had Newman or Berenger, they would have elicited a different ending from me.

"In America I held seven or eight months of screen tests: everyone was right for his part, even the beginners, that was the amazing thing. They were better than the Neapolitans. Neapolitans have to be good in order to survive; the Americans are good maybe from ignorance. We Europeans have too great a sense of the ridiculous. If I call an attorney to play the part of an attorney, he does not think of what he is like in real life but of Spencer Tracy and tries to imitate him. Nothing could be worse. But James Woods's attorney in *Once Upon a Time in America* was a real lawyer and he behaved as if James Woods were his client.

"The movie did not win an Oscar because it was not presented for one. By that time it was all over with: things had gone very badly; after ten days they had pulled it to bits. [In the United States the film appeared shortened by seventy-five minutes and re-edited in chronological order against the director's will, *Ed.*] After the failure of the shortened version, Warner Brothers ran the full version in a little movie theater outside Hollywood, just to throw me a bone, where it ran for four consecutive months. And the same thing happened in three other cities: San Francisco, Chicago and New York. They had placed all their bets on *Amadeus* which had cost 50 million dollars.

"In video-cassette it came out in both versions. The short one cost half as much. They wanted to prove to the critics that the short version was the one the public liked best. And the first week, with the short one selling for $80 and the long one $160, 2,000 were sold of the short one and 150,000 of the long one.

"Then there is the very long one that has never been edited and which lasts fifty minutes longer. Four and a half hours. But we rejected the idea of two parts on TV. It is so intricate that it

Sergio Leone with James Russo during the filming of Once Upon a Time in America.

has to be done in one evening. And besides, let's be honest: this one is my version. The other perhaps explained things more clearly and it could have been done on TV in two or three parts. But the version that I prefer is this one, that bit of reclusiveness is just what I like about it.

"And while I made a movie that I thought would please people of my generation – which it did – my greatest surprise was the enthusiasm of young people. Perhaps just because they were lacking a film of that kind... I read letters from these kids that came from all over the world. A Neapolitan youngster Marcello Garofalo, sent me a letter that gave me great pleasure, particularly coming as it did after all the critiques, and saying in part: 'The thought that the cinema has you to count on truly makes my life better.'

"A German who saw it 200 times wrote: 'For me it is not a movie, it is life.' I heard an attorney say the same thing about *Star Wars*. He told me, 'If I do not see *Star Wars* I can't manage to live. It inspires me, I'm better in court.' Robert Hossein phoned me to say that the slogan could be: 'A movie that, when you come out of the theater, you can no longer remember the person you came in with.' " (ODF '88)

Interviews conducted by Guy Braucourt (GB), Franco Ferrini (FF), Gilles Lambert (GL), Massimo Moscati (MM), Luca Verdone (LV), and Oreste De Fornari (ODF) (See Bibliography).

FILMS

Only the sets are glamorous, with their strange mixture of different periods. Conrado San Martin, Antonio Casas, Carlo Tamberlani, Roberto Camardiel.

The Colossus of Rhodes

1960

On the island of Rhodes there is a celebration, in the presence of King Xerxes, for the conclusion of the building of the Colossus, an enormous statue in human form guarding the entrance to the port. The celebration is disturbed by an assassination attempt on Xerxes.

In fact, discontent with the tyrant is spreading on the island. A group of conspirators, including the young Mirte, is trying to elicit the help of the Athenian magistrates with the good offices of the Greek hero Darius (Rory Calhoun) who happens to be on the island. But Darius is thinking only of having a rest and of courting the lovely Diala (Lea Masari), the adopted daughter of Carete, the architect who designed the Colossus.

One day, as Darius follows her through the underground passages of the palace, he involuntarily comes upon a diplomatic meeting of Xerxes, his treacherous counselor Tireus and a delegation of Phoenician pirates. Darius is discovered and suspected of spying.

For this reason Tireus refuses to allow Darius to depart so that he is forced to accept the help of the rebels and board a ship at night that is about to sail for Athens. But while the vessel is trying to slip past the Colossus, someone pulls a lever that unloads burning pitch onto it. The conspirators, who are now Tireus' prisoners, are put to cruel tortures.

Meanwhile dozens of Phoenician slaves are brought into the city and gathered at the temple of Baal. It is a trick: they are really Phoenician soldiers, allies of Tireus. He is preparing a coup to overthrow Xerxes and make Rhodes a Phoenician colony. The rebel prisoners are led before Xerxes. Diala tries in vain to convince Darius to collaborate and reveal the names of the other conspirators. When the prisoners are about to be thrown into the flaming mouth of the god, a skirmish erupts which allows them to flee on horseback and take refuge among the rocks. There they prepare to occupy the Colossus and unleash the rebellion.

Darius returns to Rhodes by night and enters Diala's room. He wakes her gently and convinces her to accompany him secretly to the Colossus where they are surprised by a group of Tireus' soldiers. Darius defends himself duelling with them and eventually, passing through one of the Colossus' ears, leaps into the sea. In reality Diala and Tireus are co-conspirators for the conquest of power. When her father, who has heard everything,

comes forward and threatens to reveal their plans, Tireus has the soldiers kill him as Diala looks impassively on. Meanwhile Darius has reached the rebels' camp, finding it destroyed and strewn with corpses.

In the arena, before Xerxes and a great crowd, the rebels are about to be thrown to the lions. Darius arrives and publicly reveals the conspiracy. At that moment a Phoenician arrow kills Xerxes: it is the start of the coup, valiantly parried by the patriots. During the fighting Darius falls prisoner to Tireus and is taken to the Colossus where Diala graciously agrees to delay his execution.

The patriots try to break through the entrance to the Colossus with battering rams, but they are repelled by Tireus' soldiers who pour boiling pitch on them.

Suddenly an earthquake strikes causing everything to collapse: scenes of panic and despair. Then a tidal wave overwhelms the Colossus.

The following day the sun shines again on the ruins of Rhodes. Darius has by now decided to remain on the island together with the honest Mirte.

* * *

Summer 1948. The Porta Portese flea market in Rome under a sudden shower. A man who works for the city pasting up posters and whose bicycle has just been stolen takes refuge under a projecting roof with his little boy and some German seminary students whose foreign tongue aggravates the man's feeling of isolation. It is a scene from *The Bicycle Thief*, at once off-hand and melodramatic, according to neo-realistic canons. Just for the record, one of the German seminary students is a certain Sergio Leone, an assistant of De Sica's, who will emerge the least neo-realistic directors of Italian cinema. This will be the destiny of a career spanning half a century of Italian filmmaking, with all its miseries and splendors.

A silent movie actress, Edvige Valcarenghi (stage name: Bice Valerian), marries a veteran film director, Vincenzo Leone (alias

Lea Massari about to betray Rory Calhoun.

Roberto Roberti) and from this union is born a son, Sergio, on January 3, 1929. The movie profession, as everyone knows, is full of uncertainties, and Signor Leone, embittered because the Fascist regime has blacklisted him, plans a respectable career as a lawyer for little Sergio. But the boy will prefer to face the sacrifices of a long artistic apprenticeship: he had, it seems, the movies in his blood.

For ten years he will be an assistant to many Italian directors (Bonnard, Camerini, Soldati, Comencini, Gallone…) and to some Americans (Wise, Walsh, Wyler, Zinnemann) who come to Hollywood-on-the-Tiber to shoot spectacular productions with the capital of their big companies frozen in Europe. (Leone had many fathers and will have many sons: Corbucci, Argento, Giraldi, Colizzi, etc. will get their start with him).

In 1959 Bonnard interrupted the scarcely initiated shooting of *Last Days of Pompeii* to return to Rome in order to direct Alberto Sordi and Vittorio De Sica in *Gastone* (one of the few decent portrayals of the Italian Belle Epoque) and entrusted the direction of the historical film to Leone.

At first glance *Last Days of Pompeii* might seem like a pale copy of the American spectacular epics about persecuted Christians, a *Quo Vadis?* without the spiritual beauty of

Deborah Kerr-Ligia and without the amusing perfidies of Peter Ustinov-Nero. But the lack of humor and the wooden acting are compensated for by certain muscular dynamics that are absent in the American models. We see Steve Reeves rip his chains out of the walls of his cell, fight with a shark in the consul's pool, and confront a lion in the arena.

The movie had phenomenal success: 830 million lire, very close to the 900 million record established the year before by Pietro Francisci's *The Labors of Hercules*. From 1958 to 1964 more than 150 of such costume films were produced. They were low-budget productions with great ambitions as spectaculars that compensated for the poverty of means with exhibitions by champions of muscle power and the eroticism of Sapphic queens, sadistic tortures and a pastiche of styles (baroque, comedy, parody, fantasy). Often they were too timid, but sometimes rather foolhardy as in Cottafavi's *Hercules and the Conquest of Atlantis*. Their success was limited to neighborhood movie houses and to certain Parisian film magazines.

Another curious fact: the cast of *Last Days of Pompeii* brings together the future fathers of the Spaghetti Western – Sergio Leone, Duccio Tessari, Sergio Corbucci and Enzo Barboni (who would direct the Trinity Films).

After this success Leone receives an offer to make his official debut in a large production where the true protagonist is not a man but a monument: *The Colossus of Rhodes*.

This time all of the Hollywood film conventions are present: duels fought while balancing on the shoulders of the Colossus, prisoners suspended above the lion pit, parties with gossip exchanged among guests at the triclinium, the poisoner who is himself poisoned, cathartic catastrophes, sensational occurrences at just the right moment (Xerxes exclaiming "as long as there is the breath of life in me..." and interrupted by an arrow piercing his breast); exquisite tortures (one prisoner has molten metal poured on his back, another is shut up in a bell and deafened). Dialogue full of solemn wishes ("I hope all Olympus is on your side"), heroic precepts ("the freedom of a people is worth six human lives"), inspired gallantries ("Women here exude a special fragrance: they seem made of sunlight"), senile pleasantries ("At your age one's sufferings are only due to women; at mine you suffer because women no longer make you suffer"). Even the hero, a down-to-earth bon vivant, is of American manufacture.

However, we are far from the great models of the genre. A comparison with *The Ten Commandments* could be instructive.

The true star is in fact a monument (Italian and French film posters).

Lea Massari and Rory Calhoun together on a triclinium.

Story elements: In the American movie, the Exodus was an indirect consequence of the jealousy of Ramses-Yul Brynner when the beautiful Nefertiti-Anne Baxter prefers Moses-Charlton Heston to him. Leone's movie lacks a central conflict and an interesting villain, the characters have almost no private concerns, the action is artificial, the about-face of the heroine gratuitous (but one must add that the script was partly re-written during the shooting).

Credibility: To make it seem that his boulders were not made of cardboard, De Mille invented a dramatic episode: the old Hebrew woman who falls during the transporting of the stones and would be crushed if Charlton Heston did not intervene to stop the work.

Leone's devices for faking big-budget scenes are more naive, e.g. the interminable final catastrophe which leaves us rather cold since the victims are all anonymous.

Glamour: Anne Baxter on board her boat tries to seduce a mud-covered and semi-nude Charlton Heston. The Italian film lacks this quality; there's an unconvincing-looking Rory Calhoun and a miscast Lea Massari, with her schoolgirl air, playing the part of the deceiving vamp. Only the film's sets are glamorous, with their strange mixture of different periods.

In short, Leone's idea of the Hollywood style was so approximate as to make one wonder what use his ten-year apprenticeship had been (which then continued when he was director of the second unit in Aldrich's *Sodom and Gomorrah,* a sorry biblical epic whose only light came from the eyes of Anouk Aimée as the perfidious, incestuous queen). Or else mythology was simply not his genre.

In fact he only found a personal style when he turned to the Western. Among other things, his first Westerns became for the public the equivalent of these gladiatorial spectacles – bloody, exciting, immoral – that his classical epics so dismally evoked.

Like a Fellinian dream. Conrado San Martin, Antonio Casas and the mouth of the god Baal, where the prisoners are to be thrown.

The first break with tradition is the hero's look,
which is very "un-Hollywood." Clint Eastwood.

A Fistful of Dollars

1964

The opening titles are shown against a background of shooting gunmen in silhouette. We are in Mexico. Two isolated huts are visible not far from the village of San Miguel. Joe, the man with the poncho (Clint Eastwood), who is riding a saddled mule, stops to drink at a well and sees a violent attack take place.

A child approaches the house where his mother, Marisol (Marianna Koch) is confined, when two thugs come out and shoo him away with kicks. One of the two is Chico (Mario Brega). The child runs to his father whom they also beat up in turn.

Joe enters the village. He is welcomed by a peasant with a crazed air, Juan de Dios. In the village square three American hired guns taunt Joe, shooting at the ground to scare the mule and him off. In the tavern in the middle of the square, the proprietor, Silvanito, tells him about the local division of power: on the one hand there are the Baxters, Americans, arms dealers; on the other hand and on the opposite side of the square are the Rojos, Mexicans and liquor dealers.

From below the windows of the Rojo house, Joe offers his services as a bodyguard. To demonstrate his abilities he commissions three coffins from the undertaker, then challenges the American hired guns who had taunted him and kills them. "I meant to say four coffins," he says, turning to the undertaker.

In the house of the Mexicans, Joe is given a hundred-dollar advance by Don Benito, the eldest of the three Rojo brothers, and then, as Chico takes him to his room, he runs into Marisol. After accidentally overhearing a discussion between Don Benito and his brother Esteban, who would like to get rid of him, Joe decides to move into the inn.

Some Mexican troops escorting a stagecoach arrive in the village. Joe, curious about who is in the stagecoach, lifts one of the curtains to peep in, but a pistol pointed at him from inside stops him.

The following morning at the inn, Silvanito explains to Joe that Ramon Rojo has taken Marisol from her family and made her his mistress. From the window the two of them watch the soldiers depart and, having become suspicious, decide to follow them.

On the banks of the Rio Bravo near the American border, Joe and Silvanito hide by a low wall and spy on the meeting between the Mexican soldiers and some U.S. Army troops who have met to exchange arms for the gold carried in the stagecoach. But these Yankees are nothing other than Esteban Rojo and his men disguised as blue jackets. The curtain of a cart is lifted and Ramon (Gian Maria Volonté) appears, the third of the Mexican brothers, holding a machine-gun. He does not leave a single survivor. The corpses of the real American troops, killed previously, are strewn on the ground to give the impression of a battle between the two troupes.

At the Rojo house Joe is introduced to Ramon. The latter announces that he has invited the Baxters to dinner to give a peaceful impression to the village since there is to be an inquiry about the Rio Bravo massacre. On hearing this news, Joe, who probably already sees himself losing his job without any more adversaries to be eliminated, decides to quit and give Don Benito back the advance he has received.

At the tavern, Joe and Silvanito get ready to leave for the river, equipped with two empty coffins.

It is evening. The Baxters start off for the dinner at their rivals' house feeling suspicious.

At the cemetery, Joe and Silvanito place two cadavers they have removed from the site of the massacre beside a tomb with their backs against the tombstone so that the two dead men look as if they are still alive.

John Baxter comes home with his wife from the dinner at the Rojos which, as the two of them comment, was held in an atmosphere of hypocritical courtesy. Joe is waiting for them. He informs them that two soldiers survived the massacre and can be found wounded at the cemetery. He takes $500 in exchange for the news.

Rojo gives him another $500 for the same information. The two clans, both alarmed by the false news, rush to the cemetery where a gun fight breaks out. The Mexicans get the better of it: besides hitting the two soldiers they thought were alive, they also capture the Baxters' son

At the same time (the two sequences are shown in parallel action) Joe stuns Chico who is guarding the Rojos' cellar and searches the premises until he finds the gold from the stagecoach hidden in a wine barrel; then he mistakenly gives Marisol a punch and carries her off.

We next see her at the Baxters' who the following day exchange her for their son, held prisoner by the Mexicans.

It is daytime. Seated on the veranda of the tavern in the center of the town, Joe watches the exchange of prisoners take place. The two hostages slowly cross the square on horses to rejoin their respective clans. Everything is going smoothly until Jesus, Marisol's little boy, comes rushing out of the tavern. The woman stops, dismounts and embraces her child. Her husband imprudently runs over to join his family. One of the Rojos' gunmen approaches to kill him, but Silvanito, threatening him with a rifle, stops him. Joe resolves the situation by telling Marisol to go back to the Rojos.

That evening the Mexicans celebrate. Joe practices target shooting at a suit of armor; Ramon joins in with his rifle, then sends Marisol away with a rough kiss. She is taken back to her house outside the village. Chico carries Joe around on his shoulders (Joe pretends to be drunk) and drops him on the bed. Left by himself, Joe now goes out through the window and rides his horse to Marisol's house where he breaks in and massacres the guards. One of these, who is only wounded, gets up and is about to shoot him in the back, when the woman screams to warn him. Then our hero throws a dagger at the survivor piercing his chest. He gives Marisol a present of some money so that she can finally get away with her family.

When he goes back to his room, Joe finds Ramon and the others there; they have discovered his trickery.

In the cellar they torture him, but he refuses to reveal Marisol's whereabouts. The Mexicans leave him lying stunned on the floor. When Chico and his companion return, intending to continue beating him up, Joe rolls a demijohn at them on the

Thriller effect. Joe sells information to the Baxters. Clint Eastwood with Margarita Lozano (above) and Wolfgang Lukschy (below).

sloping floor and makes a direct hit. Crawling on all fours he gets out and settles himself around a corner. The others arrive. Joe throws a match onto the flooded floor and causes a fire.

The infuriated Mexicans search for him everywhere and beat up Silvanito just for being his friend. Joe is hidden in the laboratory of the undertaker, who will accompany him out of the village.

The Rojos, believing Joe to be hidden at the Baxters' house, lay siege to the place. They breach the defences with dynamite, roll in some barrels of petroleum and set it afire. The Americans come out one at a time with their hands up and are mowed down by the Rojos, who have placed themselves in front of the entrance. They have no pity even for the mother who is killed as she is leaning over her dead son's body. Joe enjoys the show from his hiding place in a coffin on the undertaker's cart.

We next find him in an abandoned mine, target practicing against a sheet of iron. His torture wounds are beginning to heal.

He begins shooting again against two superimposed sheets of iron and discovers that the bullets no longer penetrate the metal.

The undertaker arrives, gives him a stick of dynamite stolen from the Mexicans and informs him that they have taken Silvanito prisoner.

In front of the inn Don Benito, Ramon and two of their men are torturing Silvanito who is hanging from a beam by his hands, when an explosion is heard. Joe appears from out of a cloud of smoke and he advances slowly goading them to shoot at his heart. But Ramon's bursts of fire only throw him to the ground. Every time our hero gets up again, unhurt. When the Mexican's rifle is empty of bullets Joe lifts his poncho revealing the metal shield that stopped the bullets and he throws it away. He pulls out his pistol, kills Don Benito and his two gunmen, cuts the cord holding up Silvanito, and then challenges Ramon to a duel – a pistol against a rifle. The two adversaries must pick their weapons up from the ground, reload them and fire. Joe proves to be the fastest one. Finally, Silvanito shoots down Esteban Rojo, who had taken up his post in a window.

Joe says goodbye to Silvanito (the gold from the stagecoach will be returned to the Mexican government) and rides off on his horse as the undertaker measures the corpses for coffins.

* * *

Westerns are as familiar and as remote as the moon. You recognize them at once, but they are not easy to define: epic style? Stoic morality? Historical? Horses and guns? All the more because it is hard to find one in its pure state; they are often mixed with melodrama or *noir* elements. And despite their American origins, for a long time they have been produced in Europe too: from the Belle-Epoque France of Joe Hamman-Arizona Bill to the Nazi Germany of Luis Trenker's *Der Kaiser von Kalifornien (The Emperor of California)*, to the Germany of the sixties of the Winnetou cycle inspired by the novels of Karl May, to Spain...

The first Italian writer of Westerns, Emilio Salgari, was a contemporary of the Lumière brothers. Starting in 1896, this highly popular writer wrote a cycle of three Western novels without ever setting foot outside Italy. Every now and then we note historical events in them. For example, in *La scotennatrice* [The woman scalper] (1909) there is a description of the Indian massacre at Sand Creek perpetrated by Colonel Chivington's troops on November 29, 1864. "The warriors were scalped, killed or wounded, the women disemboweled and their fingers cut off to get at their rings, the children's heads smashed by stones." And this, sixty years before *Soldier Blue!* But the Italian Western does not have only literary precedents. At the beginning of the century, during the European tour of Buffalo Bill's circus, the American cowboys were challenged by the Tuscan *butteri* and the rodeo challenge ended in a sensational victory of the latter.

In December 1910 the Metropolitan Opera of New York presented the world premier of Giacomo Puccini's *The Girl of the Golden West* based on David Belasco's drama. It is the love story of a saloon proprietress and an outlaw, the film abounding in manhunts, poker games, attempted lynchings and horses on the stage. There is even the blood dripping from the ceiling which leads to the discovery of the bandit as in *Rio Bravo*. More than half a century later Leone was asked to stage *The Girl of the Golden West*, but strange as it may seem, he never really liked the opera.

Between 1910 and 1949 a few Westerns were made in Italy such as Carl Koch's melodramatic *Una signora dell'Ovest* [A lady from the West] (1942) with Valentina Cortese, Michel Simon and Rossano Brazzi, and the parody *Il fanciullo del West* [The kid from the West] by Giorgio Ferroni (1943) starring Macario. One of the very first was *La vampira indiana* [Indian vampire] (1913) directed by Leone's father and starring his mother.

One cannot omit two pictures of Pietro Germi's from the list, undeclared tributaries of the Western: *In nome della legge* [In the name of the law] (1949) on the conflict between an upright and fearless judge and an old-fashioned Mafioso (on horseback); and, above all, *Il brigante di Tacca del Lupo*

The Latin roots of the Italian Western: a taste for martyrdom. Joe (Clint Eastwood) reduced to an "ecce homo."

[Brigand from Tacca del Lupo] (1952) which seems distantly inspired by *Fort Apache* in its depiction of the fight of Piedmontese blue jackets against pro-Bourbon brigands.

In 1948 the first issue of *Tex* by Bonelli and Galeppini came out, one of the most popular of the Western comic books. Exported to various European and South American countries, it is still published today. In it one finds law-abiding Indians, baroque villains à la Cagliostro, lots of people killed, and few female characters. Further to be included among the sources of the Italian Westerns are some American productions, mainly from the fifties, that helped form the taste of Leone and his followers.

First of all there is, of course, *Shane* with its white-clad hero and black-clad, taciturn villain seen through the fascinated eyes of a little boy. And then there are certain realistic details such as bullets that make the man they hit jump backwards. Other adult Westerns Leone may have remembered only for an object, a gesture, an actor's face and which he transferred to his own films denuded of any ethical historical values – the watch of the avenger in *Bravados,* the treasure hidden in the cemetery in *The Law and Jack Wade,* the long raincoats of the bandits in *My Darling Clementine,* Charles Bronson playing the harmonica in

Vera Cruz, Charles Bronson whittling a whistle in *The Magnificent Seven,* Henry Fonda giving a paralytic's crutch a kick in *Warlock;* a businesswoman who thinks of exploiting the railroad passing through her land (*Johnny Guitar*), three killers who wait for their victim at the station (*High Noon*).

And then, for the sake of completeness, we should cite the James Bond series that only just preceded Leone's Westerns and which share with them a high rate of violence combined with a low rate of emotional involvement and moral implications. Then, too, there are certain comedies of the sixties that recount the cynicism and lust for riches of Italians during the economic boom with a mixture of complicity and disapproval.

Exoticism, cynicism, melodrama, the comic-strip, parody – all these are elements that we find in the Italian Western. But the first ones were nothing but apocryphal versions of American originals where the directors used slightly fraudulent pseudonyms such as Terence Hathaway, John Fordson and Frank Garfield...

Leone enlisted in this foreign legion under the name Bob Robertson meaning "the son of Roberto Roberti." He had more imagination than his colleagues and instead of imitating the Americans, he imitated the Japanese. For *The Magnificent*

A 'holy family.' Marianne Koch, Daniel Martin with little Fredy Arco in the role of Jesus.

39

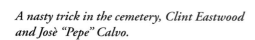

A nasty trick in the cemetery, Clint Eastwood and Josè "Pepe" Calvo.

Banquet at the Rojo's. Mario Brega and Clint Eastwood (above); Sieghardt Krupp and Antonio Prieto (below).

Seven, John Sturges drew inspiration from Kurosawa's *Seven Samurai.* Leone repeated this operation with *Yojimbo,* one of that director's distinctly minor films. *A Fistful of Dollars* is a very faithful remake of that movie. It adds to the original the massacre of the soldiers and the cemetery caper and deletes a few hold-ups and the intervention of a corrupt government official who takes bribes from both clans. But despite the almost identical subject matter, the two films have little resemblance.

The first break with tradition is the hero's appearance, which is very un-Hollywood. His unshaven cheeks and the cigarillo that hangs from his lips give him a certain squalid charm. But the impassive mask of a poker player does not hide the hard-won self control of a Bogart or a Cooper, but only the indifference of a killer. If the hero of the American Western lived on the brink between solitary adventure and the possibility of social integration, and if he took the side of the weak with a certain condescension, Leone's hero alternates incoherently between venality and gallantry. He sells himself to the highest bidder and kills for money, but he protects defenceless mothers and never shoots anyone in the back, keeping to a code of honor even stricter than that of Hollywood heroes who ride in the shadow of the Hays Office.

Above all he is astute, but in a rather mechanical, take-it-for-granted way, quite in the style of James Bond. In the following movie, in order to win the confidence of El Indio-Volonté and penetrate his gang, Clint Eastwood decides to free one of the brigand's old buddies from prison. In an American movie we would probably have been treated to an intricate episode wherein the hero gets himself imprisoned to arrange the escape, or else to become friends with the convict and extort some secret from him that will win him admission to the gang.

But Clint Eastwood chooses a quicker, easier way: he blows up the prison wall with a load of dynamite, thus allowing the prisoner to escape. Inventive storytelling was definitely out. The scene in which Eastwood sells information to the Baxters would probably have been treated by Hollywood in *noir* style. The hero is received in the boss' office in the presence of a bodyguard; an exchange of repartee, the boss is suspicious, the hero impertinent, the bodyguard looks grim and is impatient to use his fists. The boss' blonde enters and winks at the stranger... In Leone's picture there is more suspense and less humor. Mrs. Baxter comes home and goes up to her room where Eastwood, hiding in the shadows, surprises her from behind, puts a hand over her mouth and calms her down by

telling her of the rival family's intentions. The husband enters and Eastwood disarms him...

This rudimentary kind of drama is aggravated by a lack of definition (and charm) in the secondary characters: the villains who, except for Volonté are practically extras; the old tavern owner who makes us greatly miss the humor of Walter Brennan and George "Gabby" Hayes; the inexpressive mother, Marisol. Aside from the hero's cynicism, the most startling novelties are, perhaps, the nonchalance of the shoot-outs and certain *Grand Guignol-* style torture scenes.

In the American Western a too frequent use of pistols was a sign of weakness. In Samuel Fuller's *Forty Guns* and Sturges' *Gunfight at the O.K. Corral,* the sheriff advances unwaveringly on the neurotic young outlaw or the drunken cowboy without drawing his Colt, and this example of cool courage is enough to paralyze his adversary. Leone's heroes, on the other hand, are glad to show off their ballistic abilities, not against bottles, tin cans or coins thrown into the air, but directly against human beings in duels which despite the preliminary suspense (long silences, menacing looks) resemble target practice. The most original shot is taken from the viewpoint of the crackling pistol that lets us see the enemies in long-shot dropping like flies. This does not reach the sadistic refinements of the finale of *Rio Bravo* where dynamite explosions alternated with witty remarks, but to compensate there is a vague air of sportsmanship at least in the final duel pitting pistol against rifle where the winner is the one who reloads first.

The meticulous style in which the torture scenes are filmed are a milestone in the history of cinema cruelty. The giggles of the torturers, deforming close-ups of their faces, cigars squashed out on people's hands, fists emphasized during the mixing, details of the victims' swollen faces (reduced, as Leone would have put it, to an "*ecce homo*")...

The Americans were capable of greater dramatic economy. When in Anthony Mann's *The Man From Laramie* Alex Nicol has his men immobilize James Stewart and then coldly shoot him in the hand, what is most moving is the close-up of James Stewart's anguish because of the atrocity he has to undergo, rather than a detail of the wounded hand. And one can say the same of the scene where Stewart is dragged by horses.

But it is not obligatory to be allusive. Homer described with surgical precision the most lacerating blows, even if he never forgot to precede the descriptions with some genealogical details about the fallen. And there is nothing more explicit than Toshiro Mifune's body pierced by a hail of arrows in the final scene of *Throne of Blood.* But by dint of the physical, of

The meticulous care taken in the filming of torture scenes is a milestone in the history of cruelty as depicted in cinema. Antonio Prieto, Clint Eastwood, Gian Maria Volonté (above). Josè "Pepe" Calvo and Gian Maria Volonté (opposite page).

whistling arrows and of strangled cries, one reaches the point of total abstraction and the monarch ends up by resembling an impaled animal.

Leone does not have Mann's sense of proportion nor the extravagant imagination of Kurosawa. The differences between *Yojimbo* and *A Fistful of Dollars* are also primarily differences of taste. Take the hero's entrance into the village. In the former

movie a dog crosses the street holding a dead man's hand in its mouth; in the latter the corpse of a Mexican rides erect on horseback with a sign on his back saying "Adios amigo!" Kurosawa is grotesque, Leone merely smart-aleck.

Nevertheless his direction, that ranges from sweaty to self-satisfied, has not destroyed the Elizabethan seductiveness of the material: the Machiavellian intrigue, the macabre humor, the theatrical decor with the homes of the two rival families on the opposite sides of the square as on a stage. Even the archaic nature of the human relationships remains (Marisol is a kind of slave-concubine), which, if it was almost obvious in the Japanese film, is enough to give an exotic flavor to the Italian one.

When the film was released, movie buffs lamented the loss of Hollywood's laconic pistols. But the general public loved it

"When a man with a gun meets a man with a rifle, the man with the gun is a dead man." Clint Eastwood and Gian Maria Volonté, with Josef Egger in the role of the undertaker.

precisely because it did not resemble American Westerns and instead resembled the way one reinvented them in one's childhood games: a series of gunfights where the *pistoleros* never stop conceding encores. Leone has stated that what most fascinated him in the Western was "the possibility of taking justice into one's own hands: bang bang!" Even if it is not the first Western produced in Italy, it is certainly the first Italian-style Western. It is no accident that it was able to conquer both the middle – and working-class audiences, something that had not happened too often. And even more unusually, it succeeded in doing so without any kind of advertising campaign, but only by word of mouth (on this point see Tonino Valerii's testimony).

If from time to time even low-budget productions become boxoffice champions, it means that in the movie industry free competition still exists. But even free competition has its rules and regulations, first and foremost those of copyright. Someone recognized in Leone's picture a pirated remake of *Yojimbo* and the case went to court. The Japanese film's producers were awarded the exclusive distribution rights of *A Fistful of Dollars* in Japan, Taiwan and South Korea and with 15% of its commercial profits throughout the rest of the world.

Before the judge, Leone defended himself with a structuralist sally, affirming that in any case the copyright should go to Carlo Goldoni for *Harlequin, Servant of Two Masters*. Later he found a more plausible work to which to attribute Kurosawa's inspiration: Dashiell Hammett's *Red Harvest*, which is also the story of a very cunning, double-crossing avenger (a private eye in a detective agency) who cleans up a town in the clutches of gangsters by pitting one gang against the other. On a philological level it is a weak thesis (the only scene vaguely in common with the movie is the raid on the bootleggers' hide-out) however interesting it may be on a cultural one, demonstrating, as it does, how plots and clichés can travel from one continent to another with the authors being unaware of it. Leone seems to have unwittingly put a hard-boiled novel onto the screen.

Contrarily, it was excessive awareness that was responsible for making Walter Hill's terribly serious remake such a disappointment: *Last Man Standing*, with Bruce Willis in the role that had been Toshiro Mifune's and Clint Eastwood's. One feels nostalgia for the Western background that justified the provocations, reprisals and, above all, Leone's approximative style. This too played its part in making *A Fistful of Dollars* so special: a cross between American brutality, Japanese ritualism, and Roman swagger.

The public liked Leone's films because they weren't like American Westerns, but more like the way people reinvented them in their childhood games.

Almost like a Southern Italian village. Clint Eastwood and three inhabitants of Aguacaliente.

For a Few Dollars More

1965

A lone horseman is mowed down by gunfire. The opening titles appear, punctuated by pistol shots.

On a train, Mortimer (Lee Van Cleef) interrupts his Bible reading and announces his intention of getting off at Tucumcari to a petulant traveling companion. The other traveler objects that the train does not stop at that little station, but Mortimer pulls the alarm cord and the engineer stops the train precisely in the desired place.

Mortimer gets off the freight car with his horse. His authoritative appearance, fittingly emphasized by the big pistol sticking out of his belt, is enough to dampen any protests the conductor might want to make. Next to the ticket window a wanted notice is posted with a thousand – dollar reward for the capture of Guy Calloway. Mortimer tears it off and sticks it in his bag.

When Mortimer pushes the wanted notice under a door that the saloon keeper has indicated to him, he is met by a spray of bullets. He breaks into the room to find a woman in a bath tub and Calloway who is dropping down from the balcony. He goes down into the street, deploys the portable arms carrier hanging from his saddle and, with a rifle shot, slaughters the horse of the fugitive who gets up and continues firing unsuccessfully. Mortimer takes his pistol, approaches calmly, aims and shoots the bandit straight in the forehead.

Mortimer cashes in the reward in the sheriff's office where he sees a wanted notice for Baby "Red" Cavanaugh. The sheriff tells him that another bounty hunter, Monko, is on the bandit's trail at White Rocks.

At White Rocks, Monko (Clint Eastwood) enters a crowded saloon where the sheriff at his request points out "Red" who is playing poker. He breaks into the game and deals cards only to himself and the bandit. Meanwhile the sheriff sends a message to someone at the barber's. Monko wins the poker hand: "What were we playing for?" the other asks. "Our lives" says the bounty hunter disarming his foe and starting to beat him up when three men (one with his face half shaved) appear at the

door of the saloon. Monko turns suddenly and shoots them down, then killing "Red" too who, crawling across the floor, had stretched out his hand for a pistol.

He cashes in the reward from the indignant sheriff while seizing the latter's badge which he hands to two passers-by, saying: "Find yourself another one."

One night in Mexico several men attack a prison and free El Indio (Gian Maria Volonté) who, before escaping, shoots his cellmate at close range and kills the prison director while his companions take care of the guards. They leave one of them alive so he can tell the story.

A reward of $10,000 is set on the head of El Indio, dead or alive. The two bounty hunters read the notice attentively at different times and perhaps with different intentions: Monko seems attracted by the amount of money while Mortimer stares at the words "Dead or Alive."

In the brigands den, a deconsecrated church, El Indio wreaks his vengeance on the man who had had him arrested. He has his wife and child killed and then makes him fight a duel according to unusual rules: the two men can only shoot after the music box in El Indio's pocket watch has finished playing. After his easy victory, the bandit takes his ease smoking a marijuana cigarette.

In the Tucumcari bank, Mortimer gets the director to tell him which is the most solid and impregnable bank of the region: it is the El Paso bank which only a madman would dream of trying to attack.

Monko arrives in El Paso. For a small tip a Mexican waif shows him the hotel where Mortimer is lodged. Monko gets a room in the hotel facing Mortimer's by making another guest move out.

In the deconsecrated church, where Groggy's (Luigi Pistilli) men have also arrived, El Indio gets into the pulpit to announce that the safe in the El Paso bank is hidden in a piece of furniture in the director's office (which he had learned from his cellmate).

Mortimer presents himself at the bank as a possible new

customer and the director shows him the safety measures that make the bank impregnable.

Four of El Indio's men sent out to reconnoitre arrive in town. The same waif brings Monko the news.

In the saloon, Mortimer provokes one of the four (Klaus Kinski) by striking a match on his humpback and using his cigar to light his own pipe. But the bandit keeps his rage under control and leaves the saloon with his mates.

The bank employees leave work and a watchman comes in. Lying in wait outside, the outlaws time how long the watchman takes to make his rounds of the building. From his window, Mortimer watches the bandits through binoculars, while he in turn is under the surveillance of Monko's binoculars from a facing window.

Mortimer looks through the archives of the local paper and discovers from a photograph that his mysterious vis-à-vis is a noted bounty hunter.

Monko goes to see an old man, "the prophet," who is obsessed with the passing trains near his house. The prophet informs him of Mortimer's past: he is an ex-officer of the Confederate army reduced to working as a bounty hunter. Hard times.

A Chinese man enters Mortimer's room, picks up his suitcase and carries it downstairs. The ex-colonel follows him with curiosity and in the street discovers the instigator of this strange operation – Monko, who wants to get rid of his rival and orders him to leave town. A half-serious duel starts between the two rivals as the little kids watch admiringly: the men stomp on each other's feet and send bullets whizzing through each other's hair.

Having overcome their mutual mistrust, the two men converse in Mortimer's room. They decide to split the reward money and agree on a common strategy against El Indio: Monko should get himself admitted to El Indio's gang by freeing Sancho Perez, an old outlaw presently incarcerated in the Alamagordo prison. The ex-colonel loves to listen to the music box in his pocket watch, but he refuses to explain the reason for this habit to his partner.

In his hide-out El Indio smokes a marijuana cigarette while listening to the same tune played on an identical watch and remembering the circumstances in which he took possession of that object.

Flashback: A rainy evening and a young couple stretched out on their bed listen to the notes of that music box; the brigand who has broken into the room kills the husband and rips the wife's nightgown off her.

In the prison of Alamogordo, Monko blows up an outside wall and flees with Sancho Perez.

In the outlaws' den, El Indio welcomes the new recruit to the gang and gives instructions for the following day: Monko and three other men will have to set up a diversion, a robbery at the Santa Cruz bank so as to draw the sheriff's men away from El Paso. During a bivouac, Monko kills his traveling companions. El Indio and his men leave for El Paso.

In the Santa Cruz telegraph office, Monko compels the telegraph clerk to wire off the false news of the bank robbery, then ties him up and gags him.

In El Paso the colonel prepares the weapons and Monko lies in waiting among the houses facing the bank entrance. The employees leave and the watchman enters. He sits down himself in the director's office and bites into a sandwich. The Mexicans arrive in town, some on horseback, others in a covered wagon. Very soon the covered wagon disappears. Suddenly an explosion is heard – a wall of the bank has been blown up. El Indio kills the watchman and then has the piece of furniture containing the safe loaded onto the wagon. The two partners, astonished, can do nothing but rush in pursuit of him.

During a rest pause, Monko blames Mortimer for the disgrace but decides that he will continue to hunt down El Indio on his own. The ex-colonel fires on his mate without warning and gives him a flesh wound in the neck so that El Indio will not get suspicious about Monko's being the only survivor of the Santa Cruz expedition; that he has miraculously escaped a vigilantes' attack. He arrives at the bandits' camp where he proves his ability to play his role. He punches Groggy when he dares to insinuate that he is not telling the truth. El Indio, seeing the wound in his neck, believes him.

Near the village of Aguacaliente the bandits decide to test the talents of the new gunman and make him enter that inhospitable village alone. Suddenly, at the end of the street, three menacing characters take up positions. In a garden, a boy is trying in vain to reach the branches of an apple tree. Monko comes to his aid by shooting down lots of the fruit for him. Mortimer appears on the balcony of the inn and joins the target practice. Seeing this impressive display of bravura the three disappear.

Inside the saloon, the hunchback recognizes Mortimer and, to avenge the way Mortimer insulted him in El Paso, he challenges him to a duel. The ex-colonel surprises his adversary by pulling a handy Derringer out of his jacket and shoots him

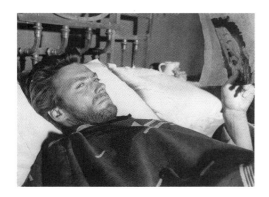

The hero (Clint Eastwood), has no scruples about asking for money, and in fact it is this venal side of the character that appeals to the public. The 'happy end' when he takes in the outlaws' bodies to claim the bounty scandalized a French critic of the Cahiers du cinéma.

straight in the forehead. Then he offers El Indio his services as a safe expert for a large sun of money.

They use sulphuric acid and Mortimer opens the safe without damaging the banknotes. El Indio closes the safe again and hides it in a hut.

At night, Monko climbs into the hut from the roof and finds Mortimer there transferring the banknotes into two sacks. Then he seals the safe in a way to make it appear that it has not been touched. Monko climbs back up through the roof and, when he is about to touch the ground, he feels the shoulders of El Indio under his feet. He just manages to throw the two sacks into the branches of a tree unseen.

The two are beaten bloody by the Mexicans. But during the night, Nino (Mario Brega), El Indio's faithful helper, after knifing another member of the gang, lets them make a getaway. Then El Indio accuses another one of his bunglers of the murder and kills him. He has a diabolical plan in mind which he confides to Nino alone: arrange for the two bounty hunters and his own helpers to kill each other and to keep the money for himself. Groggy, who has guessed what he is up to, eliminates Nino by a dagger thrust with the intention of taking his place in his chief's confidence. But the two soon are treated to the bitter surprise of finding the safe empty. While a shoot out erupts in the village streets, in which Mortimer and Monko easily come out the winners, El Indio remains seated at a table toying with a cockroach. Then he opens his watch and the music box takes him back to that famous night.

Flashback: El Indio, having shot the husband, rapes the wife. But she, while he is on top of her, gets her hand on his pistol and shoots herself in the side.

From outside Mortimer's cries of challenge can be heard. Groggy rushes out and the ex-colonel shoots him on the run. But Mortimer in turn is struck by a bullet fired by El Indio and is disarmed. El Indio challenges him to the unfair duel ("When the music stops pick up the pistol and try to shoot.").

The hero having infiltrated the brigands. **In the foreground**: *Luigi Pistilli, Mario Brega, Gian Maria Volonté, Clint Eastwood, Klaus Kinski.*

Monko intervenes and, keeping the bandit covered with his rifle, throws Mortimer a cartridge belt, thus re-establishing equality between the two duelists. They draw their pistols. Mortimer is the faster. He goes to take the other pocket watch from the bandit's body: the woman whose picture it contains is his sister, the poor suicide of that night. Mortimer renounces the reward and takes leave of his partner who is intent on loading the valuable corpses of the outlaws onto a cart. They do not add up correctly, one is missing. In fact, Groggy, who is only wounded tries to shoot Monko in the back. But the latter quickly turns and fires.

Getting the sacks from the branches of the tree, the bounty hunter moves off driving the cart loaded high with the cadavers.

*   *   *

By now it seemed that the future of the Italian cinema lay west of the Missouri. Leone had discovered a successful new genre: the Spaghetti Western. (The slightly pejorative term was coined by the American press.) In 1965 alone, thirty such movies were made. Their ingredients are well-known: much gunfighting, lots of violence, no sentimental distractions and a pinch of irony.

Other directors added some variants. In *Django,* Sergio Corbucci tried to break all records for sadism. The hero, dressed in black, travels with a coffin from which he now and then takes out a machine-gun and mows down dozens of adversaries. The bad guys are crueler than usual: when they take the hero prisoner they do not stop with beating him up, they crush his hands to a pulp under the hoofs of horses. It also has culture: a quote from *Alexander Nevsky,* with the Ku Klux Klanners swallowed alive by the mud. Everything is gratuitous, monotonous, shapeless – but at the time, the abuse of violence seemed scandalous. *Django* was the first Western to be banned to young people under eighteen and in England the censor refused to let it be shown at all.

With *Il grande silenzio* [The great silence] Corbucci established another first: the first Western where in the end the bad guy (Klaus Kinski) kills the good guy (Jean-Louis Trintignant).

In *A Pistol for Ringo,* Duccio Tessari takes the Goldonian inspiration of Leone's movie for his own. Ringo, alias Angel Face, is a double-crossing hero, infallible with a pistol, and gallant with the ladies. His adversary is a grotesque Mexican bandit who has fun decimating his hostages by making them play Russian roulette. In the background there is the flirtating between the bandit's woman and a prisoner, the aristocratic hacienda owner. The attempts at rakish comedy are compromised by a constant play of juvenile jokes. For example, in the end Ringo kills the bandit with the astuteness of a billiard player: he shoots at a bell hanging from the ceiling, calculating the trajectory of the bounce and hits his target. In compensation, Tessari does not lack ambitious cultural alibis. In a letter to the magazine *Cinema nuovo* he writes: "My Ringo is a character full of doubts, of fears, is constantly polemicizing (perhaps he is futilely anarchic, a nihilist steeped in *Sturm und Drang*) with a society which he does not accept but which, unconsciously, he wants to improve."

At the time it was fashionable, even among the literati, to discuss James Bond and the Spaghetti Western. Moravia thought that the success of the genre was the unconscious fear of over-population. The massacres carried out by Clint Eastwood and his likes were a lightning solution to the problem. Mario Soldati made free with sarcastic remarks at the expense of his ex-assistant Leone, but, curiously, he loved Giorgio Ferroni's *One Silver Dollar* because of the moving melancholy with which it represented the South after its defeat.

Leone sought more solid attractions than sadism or parody. For one thing, the quality of the faces. In the cast of his new movie *For a Few Dollars More,* along with Eastwood and Volonté, there is a little-known American character actor, Lee Van Cleef, (*High Noon, The Man Who Shot Liberty Valance*) whom Leone promoted to co-star, creating a part made to measure for his sculptural profile.

Another novelty with respect to the preceding movie is the antiquarian's taste for period firearms, reflecting a hobby widely pursued in Italy too. In addition there is a fine and studied approach to choosing locations and costumes. But most of all, the characterizations are an improvement over the earlier picture.

This time there are two heroes. Clint Eastwood has a profession: bounty hunter. In Anthony Mann's movies *(The Naked Spur and The Tin Star)* this was a rather infamous profession. Leone rehabilitates its image in order to bring the figure of the hero into line with the public's new taste, making him decidedly cynical and venal. The happy ending which sees him load the outlaws' corpses onto a cart, not to take them for

*An act of provocation not easily
forgotten: Lee Van Cleef striking a match
on the hump of hunchback Klaus Kinski.*

burial but to cash in the reward, even scandalized a critic of the *Cahiers du cinéma*.

The other hero, Colonel Mortimer, is an all Bible-and-pistol type whose self-control hides bellicose intentions of vengeance. The villain is a manic depressive with self-destructive tendencies.

The moral of the American Western was often based on a compromise between free will and predestination. For example, Borden Chase's friendly enemies (in *Bend of the River* and *Vera Cruz*) are free to choose between good and evil, to yield to or resist the temptations strewn along their paths, even if it is easy to guess right from the start what their choices are going to be.

Leone adopts a more elementary Manicheism. His heroes have faces like primitive masks. It is enough to see what they smoke to guess at their characters. The pipe of the colonel, sign of a stubborn and reflective temperament; the short cigar of Monko which gives him his couldn't-give-a-damn air; the marijuana cigarette that explains El Indio's hallucinatory look.

One of the movie's themes is the celebration of vengeance according to a Latin and melodramatic tradition. This will be a constant in the Spaghetti Western.

In American Westerns, vengeance is often expressed euphemistically. The hero has to eliminate the villain because he is a danger to society besides being guilty of having killed the

The villain, the most imaginative of the three, is a cyclothemic Mexican attracted to acts of self-destruction. (Gian Maria Volonté).

hero's friend (the case of *My Darling Clementine,* among others). Sometimes, as in *Bravados,* a Catholic Western by Henry King starring Gregory Peck, vengeance is openly condemned both during the story and in the finale, when he learns that he was mistaken: the men he killed were not those who murdered his wife.

More interesting are some auteur Westerns, such as *The Searchers* or *Rancho Notorious,* where vengeance rather than being condoned or condemned, is transcended by an epic or tragic catharsis. In Ford's film, John Wayne's tenacious hatred of Indians sometimes appears unjust or even absurd, but it is also fatally inscribed in the collective destiny of the conquerors. In Lang's picture, Arthur Kennedy joins forces with the outlaws to find his fiancée's killer, but hatred turns him into a cynic ready to use the love of a woman for the purposes of his vengeance. So he too becomes the victim of a universal destiny of guilt.

Leone limits himself to wrapping the story of vengeance in a Gothic novel atmosphere. Brigands straight out of a court of miracles (hunchbacks, giants, scarfaces...), rape photographed

through a rose-colored lens, a close-up of the dead woman that brings Poe to mind... Furthermore the tragic event is divided up into two flashbacks in the style of the psychoanalytical melodrama (*The Snake Pit, Marnie*) and we cannot exclude the possibility that it may have left traumas on the two antagonists. In fact the bandit has a strange compulsion to recall it by listening to the music box set in his watch which is identical to the colonel's (even with its own music box and same music). Thus is the operatic style of the subsequent movies announced.

It is in the duels that Leone reveals his taste for the

Bounty hunters. Clint Eastwood and Lee Van Cleef.

ceremonial. If, such as Hawks, Ford and Mann are concerned about the right dosage of gunfights and about motivating their presence in the story, what seems to interest Leone is mainly to vary the protocol each time. There is the upshot in the deconsecrated church when El Indio takes revenge on a traitor; the semi-serious duel where the two heroes shoot holes in each other's hats under the ecstatic gaze of a group of urchins; the target practice scene where the two bring down a shower of apples to the joy of a little Mexican child; the final clash, with the arena and referee. What is new about these duels is that, since they are rituals, they can be enjoyed both as drama and as parody.

There is an ambiguity which does not regard the film as a whole (weighed down, among other things, by the excessively long robbery episode) but which suffice to make Leone recognized as an unconscious heir of the great mannerist painters, capable of re-designing a traditional subject in an up-to-date and slightly disenchanted way. As in the paintings of that period there is a kind of portrait of the patron which here becomes a pretext for a little private vendetta. In the grotesque guise of the innkeeper, a woman of easy virtue, and her small, nasty-looking husband, it seems we are asked to recognize the wife of a producer who, once upon a time, had not behaved entirely correctly towards Leone.

The Good, the Bad and the Ugly   1966

The opening titles appear superimposed on daguerrotype-style photos. Three killers enter a saloon. Explosions. Tuco (Eli Wallach) comes tumbling out through a window, shattering the glass: in one hand he holds a pistol, in the other a steak bone. The image freezes and the caption "The Ugly" appears. While Tuco gallops off we see that two of the killers in the saloon are dead. The third, with a wounded arm, tries to shoot at the fugitive, but he cannot manage it and falls to the ground.

A horseman, Angel Eyes (Lee Van Cleef), enters a lonely farmhouse and sits down to lunch with the head of the family. He asks him for news of Corporal Carson who escaped some

time back with the safe of a Confederate regiment. The owner of the house, frightened, gives him the information and begs him to spare his life, offering him double what he is getting to kill him. Angel Eyes takes the money but kills him and his two sons anyway, sparing only the widow. The instigator of the crime, who is in bed with a violent cough, pays off Angel Eyes. The latter explains that the victim had paid him more and so he wipes him out by shooting him in the head through a cushion. The image freezes and the caption appears: "The Bad."

In a rocky place, three bounty hunters are waiting to ambush Tuco who has a reward of $2,000 on his head. Along comes

The Good. Clint Eastwood.

Blondie (Clint Eastwood) and kills them. Now Blondie takes Tuco, tied and mounted backwards on a horse, to the town, delivers him to the sheriff and cashes in the reward. He is about to be hanged on the village square after a functionary has read publically the list of his many crimes. From a rooftop Blondie shoots down the hanging rope and the hats of the bystanders to facilitate the bandit's escape.

The two of them meet far from the village and split the reward money. In another town they successfully repeat the trick. Angel Eyes, who is passing through town, watches the scene as a legless Confederate war veteran tells him that if he wants information about Carson he will have to see his woman Maria, a prostitute.

Blondie, since the reward on his accomplice's head does not appear to be increasing, abandons him tied up in the middle of the desert. The image freezes and the caption appears: "The Good."

A group of drunken Confederate soldiers let Maria get off a wagon. Entering her house, the woman finds Angel Eyes lurking in the shadows; he beats her to make her tell him where Carson is.

After an exhausting march in the desert, Tuco reaches a village and quenches his thirst at a horse trough. Then he goes crashing into an emporium and makes the old proprietor show him his entire stock of pistols. After long examination he puts together a weapon composed of three pieces taken from various arms and tries out the new pistol in the courtyard, demonstrating his extraordinary aim. Then he goes off, but not before having emptied the shop's cash register.

The Confederate troops are retreating to a small town. In a hotel three of Tuco's killers steal up the stairs to Blondie's room where he is cleaning a pistol. But despite the noise of the passing troops, the bounty hunter does not miss the sound of their spurs and he greets the Mexicans with three well-placed shots. All in vain, since Tuco enters from the window at his back, surprising him and ordering him to hang himself from a roof beam. Blondie already has the rope around his neck when a cannon shot makes the floor give way and Tuco finds himself on the floor below. Above, the rope is still tied to the beam, but of Blondie there is no trace.

Angel Eyes reaches a half-destroyed fort where some Confederate soldiers have found refuge. At the end of their strength, they are boiling some corn cobs. The bandit questions them on the whereabouts of Bill Carson. They answer that if he is not dead he must have ended up in the Union prison camp at Betterville.

Tuco, who has gone in pursuit of Blondie reaches the bivouac that his rival has shortly abandoned. A cigar stub, still lighted, is the sure sign he has been there.

Blondie is about to perform one of his usual last-minute rescues from the gallows with a new partner, Shorty. But Tuco, coming upon him from his back, points his pistol and orders him

to leave his accomplice to his fate.

Tuco announces his vendetta: he is going to make Blondie cross the desert on foot, and to make it harder he shoots his hat off and shoots holes in his water bag.

Blondie, exhausted, makes his way among the dunes, his face scorched by the sun, accompanied by Tuco who protects himself under a parasol.

During a rest stop, Tuco washes his feet in a tub. Blondie, dying of thirst, crawls over on all fours, but the other, kicks over the tub with a scornful laugh. Prostrate, Blondie rolls down a dune. He does not have the strength to get up again and the other is just pointing his pistol at him to wipe him out, when the sound of hoofs announces the arrival of a stagecoach without a driver.

Inside it are the corpses of some Confederate soldiers from which Tuco pilfers the money and valuable objects. One of these soldiers, still in his death agony, is the famous Corporal Carson who, in exchange for a drink of water, reveals the secret that the regiment's cash box is buried in the cemetery of Sad Hill. Before telling him the name on the tomb, Carson demands that Tuco bring him the water bag. The latter goes off for a moment to get it, and on his return discovers that Carson has already died and has given the precious revelation to Blondie. So now it is in Tuco's interests to let him live.

Disguised in Corporal Carson's uniform (including his black eye-patch) Tuco drives the stagecoach, looking for a place where Blondie can be given medical treatment. At a Confederate block point they tell him that the only infirmary is in the Mission of San Antonio.

There the monks take Blondie under their care. Tuco, to get the tomb name out of him, deceives him about the condition of his health, insinuating that he is not going to make it. But his old partner is too cagey to fall into the trap and reacts by throwing a coffee cup at him.

Blondie is better by now. Before they leave, Tuco meets a brother of his, a monk (Luigi Pistilli) who reproves him for his sordid career of banditry.

Back on the march, the two, who are dressed in Confederate uniforms, meet up with a cavalry company. Tuco greets them joyously, singing hymns of praise to the Confederacy. Too late he realizes that their gray uniforms are in reality blue ones covered in dust.

They end up in the Union prison camp of Betterville. Tuco, who has assumed the identity of Corporal Carson, is late to answer roll call getting himself a punch in the stomach from the gigantic Corporal Wallace (Mario Brega) and arousing the suspicions of a sergeant who is no other than Angel Eyes.

The commander of the camp, forced by a gangrenous leg to be inactive, reproves him harshly for pilfering from the prisoners. Angel Eyes invites Tuco to lunch in his lodgings. After some initial diffidence, Tuco eats greedily. Seeing that the

*The cruelty of the three adventurers is
set against a backdrop of the horrors
of war.*

Mexican is playing dumb concerning the fate of the real Carson, Angel Eyes goes on to more persuasive measures. He crushes his finger in a tobacco box and has the corporal torture him while an orchestra composed of prisoners plays loudly to cover the Mexican's screams. At last, Tuco reveals the name of the cemetery where the treasure is buried.

Now it is Blondie's turn, but Angel Eyes, who despairs of being able to make him talk by torture, leaves with him for the cemetery of Sad Hill. The deal is that they are to split the treasure two ways.

The corporal takes Tuco to the train for the city where he must deliver the outlaw to the authorities and rake in the reward.

Blondie and Angel Eyes are sleeping where they have camped for the night. Blondie, awakened by a suspicious rustling sound, shoots and hits a man hidden among the trees. At Angel Eyes' signal, his five stooges pop out of the woods and join the leads in the treasure hunt.

Tuco is traveling in a cattle car hand-cuffed to Corporal Wallace. At a certain point he asks his permission to urinate out of the car and takes advantage of the occasion to leap from the moving train, dragging the soldier with him. Then Tuco knocks his head against a rock, killing him.

To free himself from the handcuffs, he places the corpse between the railroad tracks so that a passing train will cut the chain.

Blondie and Angel Eyes reach a town which has been half destroyed by bombardments while a column of Union soldiers is passing through. Tuco, too, is in town, immersed in a bubble bath in a ruined hotel. An old enemy of his (the guy who lost an arm in the opening shoot-out) comes in to kill him, but the Mexican is faster and shoots him with a pistol hidden among the bubbles.

Blondie recognizes the unmistakable explosion and arrives intending to renew his old partnership with him. Out in the streets the two comrades get the better of Angel Eyes's men thanks to their team-work and the smoke raised by the cannonades. But the gang leader manages to escape.

Along a wilderness trail, Blondie and Tuco, stopped by a Union patrol, are taken to the trenches alongside a river: the Confederates are installed on the other side of the river. A captain who is a whisky lover and a war hater (Carlo Giuffré) complains about the indifference with which the high military command sends thousands of soldiers to be massacred just for the sake of taking the Langstone Bridge.

One of the daily battles begins in which, under the cover of an artillery barrage, hundreds of soldiers invade the bridge to fight in a bloody hand-to-hand battle. The captain is seriously wounded. The two adventurers, whom only the river separates from the treasure, decide to make short shrift of the situation and, with the captain's blessing take advantage of a cease-fire to mine the bridge. Each of them reveals his secret – that is, the name of the cemetery and of the tomb (that of a certain Stanton) and light the fuse. On hearing the explosion, the captain dies in peace.

After spending the night in a ditch, sheltered from the bombardment, Tuco and Blondie wake up to find the whole area evacuated. Only the corpses testify to the previous day's battle. They wade across the river. Among the ruins of a small church Blondie comforts a dying Confederate soldier. He covers him with his cloak and gives him a cigar. Tuco takes advantage of this to go off on horseback, but the other one stops him with a gun shot.

On falling, the Mexican tumbles against a tombstone and finds that he is in the immense Sad Hill cemetery.

After an exhausting search he discovers Stanton's tomb and begins digging with his hands. Blondie is behind him and throws him a shovel. Angel Eyes too appears holding a pistol, throws Blondie a shovel and orders him to dig. But in the grave all they find is a skeleton.

Blondie had lied. Now he scratches the name of the real grave on a potsherd and places it at the center of a stony circle. The three of them stand on the edge of the circle and prepare to hold a three-way duel. They stare at each other, leer, and challenge each other than draw their pistols in a flash. The blonde guy kills Angel Eyes who tumbles into the open grave while Tuco realizes that his pistol is not loaded – his partner unloaded his pistol when he was not looking.

There is nothing scratched on the potsherd at the center of the circle; in fact, the treasure is found in the unmarked grave next to Stanton's. Tuco digs, finds the the bags of gold and exults, but he has a bad surprise in store.

And here he is now standing on a creaky wooden cross with a rope around his neck while Blondie rides off beyond the horizon after having placed half the loot at the foot of the cross. He reappears, rifle in hand, and shoots through the rope with infallible aim. Tuco falls face-first into the gold. The picture freezes and there appears the caption "the Ugly", followed in turn by "the Good" and "the Bad" (in the grave). It ends with Tuco shouting a colorful insult at his disappearing partner.

Principal scenes cut in the Italian release version

After the hold-up in the armory, Tuco recruits three accomplices to wipe out Blondie.

Tuco, on Blondie's track, reaches a village on the Mexican border where the Confederates are trying to recruit poor peons. Full of pity, Tuco takes up a collection. He enters a saloon and discovers that Blondie is upstairs in bed with a woman. Blondie then makes a spectacular escape, taking the collection money with him.

In 1966 *A Man and a Woman* wins the Palme d'or, the Oscar, and is a boxoffice success. It is the first time this has happened with a film shot according to some of the aesthetic principles of the *nouvelle vague*, full of dreams, flashbacks and documentary-style scenes. The audiences continue to be moved when the lovers meet again at the station. But if their embrace is shot with a hand-held camera and moreover in black and white, it is doubly moving for spectators to discover that they themselves have a taste for poetry. Rather than experimental films, it must have been television and its commercials that created this mass aestheticism.

After the commercial success of *Juliet of the Spirits* in Italy even average films were made with rather Byzantine wrappings. Among the box-office hits of the season there is *L'armata Brancaleone* [The Brancaleone Armada] a burlesque saga recited in archaic Italian, which would have expected to appeal only to well-educated audiences, and *Africa addio!*, Jacopetti's reportage-fiction in *Mondo cane*-style, where lyricism and truculence are cleverly mixed to serve the author's nostalgia for colonialism.

Meanwhile they continue to shoot Westerns, fifty movies – twenty more than in 1965. Even intellectuals promenade on the Main Streets of Cinecittà, armed with good intentions. Pier Paolo Pasolini plays the part of a revolutionary priest in Carlo Lizzani's *Requiescant* (the hero, also a semi-priest, is Lou Castel, of *Fist in His Pocket*). Tinto Brass shoots *Yankee* in the manner of underground comic books with close-ups of napes of necks, cigar-smoking belly buttons, nude ladies tied to poles; and the producer throws it out of the editing studio. Giulio Questi's *Django Kill!* is inspired by the director's experiences as a partisan fighter during WW II (the bandits in black uniforms represent Fascism). It is sequestered because of certain excessively violent scenes, including one depicting the rape of a young boy.

Leone prepares an international spectacular production (United Artists comes up with half a million dollars as an advance on half the boxoffice takings abroad). It is *The Good, the Bad and the Ugly*. What is spectacular about it is the setting of the American Civil War, with its many extras and cannons. The casting adds Eli Wallach to the usual Eastwood and Van Cleef. Vincenzoni, Age and Scarpelli are selected to write the script, specialists of the Italian comedy. The idea was to remake *The Great War* as a Western.

The irony in Leone's movie begins with the title. If *the Bad* is a hired killer, *the Good* is merely a bounty hunter and *the Ugly* a kind of likeable picaresque brigand. But while the Bad kills for money in cold blood, the Good only shoots to defend himself after having challenged his adversary, and the Ugly tries to kill for vengeance, but never succeeds. (He is about to shoot the Good when the phantom carriage arrives, and he is about to hang him when a providential cannonade makes the ceiling fall.) Despite everything, the stereotypes remain – without stereotypes, no irony. But it is brought up to date and gets complicated. The Good and the Ugly are distinguished from the Bad inasmuch as they are economic animals: they are capable of stipulating contracts and respecting them. On the other hand the Bad, once having killed on commission, eliminates his patron as well. The Good and the Ugly form a partnership to trick sheriffs and then become allies in hunting for the treasure, ready to betray each other as soon as the occasion calls for it, but also ready to punish the treacherous partner; and to punish him they try to hang him.

In the American Western, from Wellman's *The Ox-Bow Incident* to Ted Post's *Hang'em High,* there is much democratic disdain for lynching (in general it is the innocent who pay the

A film whose irony begins with its title. If the Bad is a hired assassin, the Good is nothing more than a bounty hunter and the Ugly, a likeable picaresque brigand. Left: The Bad, Lee Van Cleef. Right: The Ugly, Eli Wallach.

price) and a bit of nostalgia for quick procedures. In Howard Hawks's *Barbary Coast,* the San Francisco vigilantes try the killer, Brian Donlevy, while they are conducting him to the gallows in an atmosphere of ferocious judicial mirth. Leone takes up this myth with a certain taste for the absurd. His *pistoleros* send their enemies to meet their creator without much ado ("If you gotta shoot, shoot and shut up" opines the Ugly), but when it comes to punishing the partner who has violated the contract, they imitate the justice of the State and its liturgies: they compel him to make long forced marches in the desert, or, rope in hand, order him to hang himself. One would think the whole penal code had been invented by two brigands who were supposed to divide some loot.

At times it seems like a Gothic tale where all the characters have fun betting their necks against the devil. (In the prologue we see the Good deliver up the Ugly to the sheriff, cash in the reward and then, at the last moment, save him from the gallows.) As in dreams, one falls but does not die. And like the heroes in silent comedies, who avoid falling into puddles, and Hitchcock's innocents who escape plunging to their deaths, so in Leone's movie the executions are failures. At one and the same time there is a parody of the castrating law and the castration of parody: the shadow of the gallows continues to menace even if the heroes are practically immortal.

In the background is the war, the American Civil War in which Ambrose Bierce set his cruel stories. In American pictures (including Peckinpah's), Southerners are always gentlemen and Northerners self-made men; in Leone the desert dust confounds the uniforms and perhaps the centuries as well. One sees trenches, concentration camps. One hears pacifist slogans. At fixed times, hundreds of men hurl themselves upon each other to take a bridge whose strategic importance they do not understand. Leone says he was inspired by Lussu the Italian author of a novel on World War I), but Ford portrayed with more depth military grandeur and stupidity – (the suicidal charge of the Confederates in *The Horse Soldiers*).

This way of fictionalizing history is also very European. In American Westerns history is given a moral with the help of star-appeal. In Raoul Walsh's *They Died With Their Boots On,* it would seem that the Indian wars were provoked by the trader Arthur Kennedy's envy of the handsome general Errol Flynn. From the way in which the liberal Gary Cooper and the slaver Howard da Silva dispute the favors of Paulette Goddard in De Mille's *Unconquered,* one can deduce the causes of the American Revolution; and in Robert Aldrich's *Vera Cruz,* the Mexican revolution against Maximilian is legitimized by the fact that Gary Cooper takes the side of Juarez and Burt Lancaster that of the French – a Manicheism that does not exclude a certain malicious fun (in general villains and bad causes do have their fascination). In Leone there is no connection between history and how it is fictionalized. The three adventurers change uniforms with the same nonchalance as Buster Keaton in *The General*. And if they blow up a bridge, thus determining the outcome of a battle, it is only so they can continue to hunt for treasure. They go through the war with the indifference and greed of the lovers in *Senso*. But if in *Senso* when a door is opened by mistake one surprises plotting patriots (that is, history in the making) rather than a lovers' tryst; here one opens the wrong trunk and discovers the skeleton of a soldier. *Memento mori* is Leone's only message.

Only once does one gather that war is a kind of organized banditry. When the Ugly is tortured by the Bad in the barracks of a Union camp, the prisoners' band has to play louder to cover his screams – a use of the chorus that would not have displeased Brecht.

A propos of Brecht, one knows that Leone's heroes are moved by no other ideal than to get rich (someone baptized his first Westerns as "the dollar trilogy"). In this movie more than all the others, Leone recounts their rapacity with a black humor reminiscent of von Stroheim (Tuco handcuffed to the corpse of the corporal) and goes as far as to associate money and corpses with a rather sacrilegious twist. In *For a Few Dollars More* the hero adds up the amount of the rewards he will cash in as he loads the corpses onto a cart. In *The Good, the Bad and the Ugly*

the treasure map is found in a diligence full of corpses and the box of dollars buried in a military cemeter

Here too are Gothic allusions, and possible Freudian readings can be made (the corpse as a source of profit reminds one of the symbolic equivalence of money and feces). But, in Hollywood, corpses were taboo, or almost so. At the end of Anthony Mann's *The Naked Spur,* James Stewart, bounty hunter on occasion, pulls the body of Robert Ryan out of the river in order to cash in the reward for him; but a horrified Janet Leigh induces him to desist from this impious commerce. Even a totally unscrupulous outlaw like Hugh Marlowe in *Rawhide* flames with contempt when one of his companions (Jack Elam) transports the cadaver of one of his victims by dragging it behind the horse rather than loading it onto the animal's back. And not even the feelings of vengeance for the Indians nourished by the hero of *The Searchers* can justify the profanation of a grave or a dead man's eyes.

Apparently there is no taboo on dollars. And yet, normally, there figure in Westerns a capital that is morally justified for its civilizing function (land and herds) and by the risks one must run to make it multiply (Indians, landholders, thieves). *Red River* dedicates ten minutes to the building up of a cattle empire and two hours on its defence. Dollars only appear at the poker table: an intelligent hobby (Henry Fonda in *My Darling*

The desert dust creates a confusion of uniforms and also perhaps of centuries. Eli Wallach, Mario Brega, Lee Van Cleef in the prisoner camp.

Opposite: *The scene of Eli Wallach and Mario Brega jumping from the train, filmed by Tonino Delli Colli and Sergio Leone. The image of "the Ugly" handcuffed to the corpse of his jailer is reminiscent of Eric Von Stroheim's* Greed.

Clementine) but a rather shady profession (gamblers often cheat).

Sometimes money suggests sexual symbolism. In *Man Without a Star* the attractive cattle queen Jeanne Crain hires Kirk Douglas as an overseer and asks him to name his price: he imperiously writes *"You"* in the accounts book – they will end up in bed together. In George Cukor's *Heller in Pink Tights,* Sophia Loren, a gambler momentarily broke, offers herself as the stake when the betting gets heavy. This sudden turning of the female body into money seems to free it from the cage of mere representation (on the screen the nude body of a woman is still only an image of a nude woman). For a moment one has the impression that naming the price is the same as possessing the woman.

In Leone's erotic world, a dollar does not buy land, herds or girls, but perhaps it dispenses tactile pleasures and in any case it inspires a perverse kind of mysticism. The Ugly rushes to the cemetery accompanied by celestial music; he slits open the dollar sacks with blows of his spade shot from below; he rummages for spoils in the pockets of rotting corpses... Here the dollar appears in all its macabre splendor, *stercus diaboli,* which alludes to the vanity of all the galloping rides and treasure hunts of this world.

It is a fine cocktail, mixing Carnival and Lent, even if diluted by too much repetition. And it is a very free re-make of *The Great War*. Monicelli had portrayed the instinct for self-preservation by mixing comedy, realism and drama. In Leone the art of getting by becomes greed and the law of the jungle; the tragic sense approaches the taste for the macabre; realism becomes naturalism and the comic borders on the trivial. Tuco, the Ugly, wanting to leap from the train, asks the corporal if he can go and pee. The peeing man will become a recurring figure in Leone's movies.

According to Leone, the filmmaker based his film upon a book by Italian writer Emilio Lussu, which was a chronicle of life in the trenches during World War I.

A hero at twilight and a nation on the move. Cheyenne (Jason Robards), the wise brigand, rides, fatally wounded, along the railroad tracks with its workers, among whom some Chinese immigrants.

Once Upon a Time in the West

1968

As the opening titles appear, three shady types wearing long leather coats who work for a certain Frank are silently waiting for the train to arrive at the tiny desert station of Little Corner. Only one passenger gets off, Harmonica (Charles Bronson) who confronts the three and shoots them down in a flash, but falls himself with a shoulder wound.

On the isolated Sweetwater Farm, Ed McBain (Frank Wolff), an Irish widower, and his two children are preparing a banquet to welcome the bride-to-be who is arriving from New Orleans. Suddenly firing is heard and they are shot down one after the other. Five bandits emerge from the bushes led by Frank (Henry Fonda) who does not even have pity on the lone survivor, a child, and shoots it dead.

At the Flagstone station passengers get off a train, among them Jill (Claudia Cardinale), McBain's bride-to-be.

We next see her in the wagon of Sam (Paolo Stoppa), a crusty old man nostalgic for the primitive Old West, riding through the crowded streets of Flagstone. They cross the railway yard, then Monument Valley.

They stop in a tavern. Shortly, Cheyenne (Jason Robards) makes his appearance, a bandit still in handcuffs who has just shot his guards. From a shadowy corner comes the sound of a harmonica: it is Harmonica. Cheyenne provokes him without getting a reaction. The bandit has to make do with scaring a customer and making him cut the chain of his handcuffs with a gunshot as he keeps him covered by his own pistol to avoid any surprises. Cheyenne's men arrive in leather coats. The explanations they give to Harmonica make us realize that this is a kind of uniform for their gang – that is why the three thugs at Little Corner, Frank's henchmen, were wearing them as a trick.

Sam and Jill arrive at the farm where the small group of guests for the wedding feast are gathered in silence around the corpses of the McBains laid out on the tables outside the house. Jill explains that the wedding ceremony has already taken place in New Orleans.

Once the burial is over, a strip of leather coat is found which is immediately taken as evidence of Cheyenne's guilt.

Alone in the house, Jill searches nervously in the drawers and chests and then, fully dressed, stretches out on the large matrimonial bed.

In a Chinese laundry Harmonica manhandles the proprietor,

the unctuous Wobbles, who has ordered the three killers, on Frank's behalf, to kill Harmonica at the Little Corner station.

At the farm, Jill has just found several wooden models of public buildings in the drawers when she hears the familiar sound of a harmonica playing outside. She turns out the light, takes a rifle and shoots at a little flame that is shining in the night, but the sound of the harmonica does not stop.

The following morning the ground in front of the house appears to be deserted. Jill opens the door and suddenly Cheyenne appears heading a gang of his men. He does not appear to be contemplating any harm as he enters alone protesting his innocence for the McBain massacre. But he does not know who was responsible for it.

In a luxurious private car the owner of the railroad, the paralytic engineer Morton (Gabriele Ferzetti), reproves Frank for having gone far beyond his mandate by killing the McBains while not managing to stop, among other things, the appearance of a McBain widow on the scene. The bandit is inclined to violent methods and disdains the businessman. The latter, despite his hurry to reach the Pacific, eliminating all obstacles along his path, does not tire of telling Frank that money is the strongest weapon.

Meanwhile, back on the farm, Jill's candor and her talent as a cook have won Cheyenne's trust. He takes his leave politely.

In the stable Jill is getting ready to load the baggage on the wagon when Harmonica appears and orders her brusquely to stay. He begins to rip off her clothes, then orders her to go to the well. The disarray of Jill's clothes and her routine activities at the well distract two killers on horseback who have probably come to get rid of the widow. Harmonica draws his gun with lightning speed and mows them down while Cheyenne watches with satisfaction from a hilltop.

At the Chinese laundry Jill tells Wobbles she wants to talk to Frank. Wobbles denies knowing him, but then goes out, apparently exhausted. Harmonica follows him at a distance.

Wobbles arrives at Morton's private car and tells Frank of Jill's visit. Frank notices that Harmonica is hiding on the roof of the train and orders the engineer to leave.

The train stops in the middle of the desert as Frank's men arrive on horseback. After killing Wobbles with three pistol shots because he incautiously allowed himself to be followed to

The clock is an optical illusion as well as a wink at cinema buffs and recalls Fred Zinnemann's **High Noon.** *Henry Fonda.*

the train, Frank stops Harmonica and asks him his name and what he wants. He gets no reply. Harmonica remembers something (in flashback) very vaguely. Frank leaves on horseback for the McBain farm.

On the moving train Cheyenne, hiding out on the roof, eliminates the three bandit bodyguards with some clever maneuvering and frees Harmonica.

At the farm Jill receives a delivery of a large amount of wood that her husband has ordered. No one knows what it is to be used for, but the woman remembers a wooden model with the word "station" written on it. She is rummaging around in the storeroom when a hand offers her the what she is looking for: it is Frank's hand.

In front of the entrance to a cavern, the bandits' hide-out,

Morton advises Frank not to kill the woman prisoner, but the latter seems mainly interested in humiliating his partner, even knocking him to the floor by kicking at his crutches.

At the farm, Harmonica tells Cheyenne about McBain's project of building a station which, according to the terms of the contract, should be operating when the railroad arrives. The two of them begin hammering in stakes so that Jill will find the job completed on her return.

In the bandits' hide-out Frank is in bed with Jill who, with her amorous skills (in New Orleans she worked as a prostitute), probably is hoping to get him to spare her life.

In Flagstone the sheriff is auctioning off the McBain farm with the consent of the widow who is present. Frank's men intimidate the aspiring buyers.

On the train Morton is contemplating a picture of the Pacific Ocean, the supreme goal of all his efforts. Then, joining Frank's men who are playing poker, he distributes banknotes rather than cards.

In the meantime the auction has reached the moment of truth and the farm is about to be sold at a ridiculously low price to Frank's representative. At the top of the stairs Harmonica appears covering Cheyenne with his pistol. The brigand, with a big reward on his head, is Harmonica's bid. A horseman departs from Morton's railway car.

The sheriff and his helpers escort Cheyenne to the train for Yuma where there is a well-known penitentiary. The bandit's henchmen are already casing the site.

In a deserted saloon Jill is reassured by Harmonica who, in fact, is restoring her property to her. While she is going up the stairs, Frank vainly tries to buy the farm from Harmonica and to get him to give his name. The latter has another flash of memory, a little clearer than the previous one, where he sees Frank in his youth.

On the floor above, where Jill is taking a bath, Harmonica, indifferent to her charms, is on the balcony keeping track of Frank's movements (who is cautiously wandering in the deserted streets shooting at Morton's killers in ambush on the roof tops). Harmonica joins in the action, personally eliminating several killers and sending fast signals to Frank. This strange behavior puzzles the widow.

Frank reaches the private train stopped in the desert. There is no sign of life. Corpses are strewn inside and outside the train. A little farther off, Morton is dying near a puddle.

The railway work site has by now reached the vicinity of the McBains' property where the station is almost fully built. Harmonica is leaning against a wooden fence whittling a piece of wood when Frank arrives, determined to discover who he is and challenge him to a duel.

From within the house Jill and Cheyenne observe the scene. The duellists, about to begin combat, stare long at each other and Frank tries to position the other with the sun in his eyes. Harmonica has a clear recollection.

Flashback. Frank and his henchmen have put a rope around a man's neck, attaching it to a stone arch. To prolong the agony they have balanced him on the shoulders of a boy in whose mouth they have stuck a harmonica. The boy falls exhausted in the dust and the other, having lost his support, breaks his neck. That adolescent was Harmonica, the hanged man his brother.

Return to the present. The duellists draw and fire, Frank spins round and falls to the ground. Dying, Frank asks: "Who are you?" and Harmonica for an answer sticks the harmonica into his mouth. With that act the bandit before dying may remember the long-forgotten episode.

Harmonica enters the house, takes his things, and departs. Cheyenne too takes his leave – a little bitterly because he would have been glad to stay if Jill had asked him to. But the woman was only attracted by the mysterious harmonica player, who, for his part, did not seem to notice her at all.

The two adventurers are not far from the house when Cheyenne drops to the ground, thus revealing that Morton had shot him from behind during the shoot-out on the train. He begs his friend not to watch him as he dies.

The credits come up across the scene of Harmonica on horseback disappearing into the distance, carrying the body of Cheyenne.

Principal scenes cut in the Italian release version

On arriving in Flagstone, Jill offers Sam two banknotes if he will take her to Sweetwater in his wagon.

Harmonica is lying on a bed in a room above Wobbles' laundry. The proprietor's wife, a beautiful Mexican woman, enters and offers herself to him. He asks her to massage his feet, which she does. Suddenly the woman's two capable hands are replaced by the two strong hands of a man. Harmonica has no time to react. Three tough guys begin beating him up and push him into a stable where the sheriff is waiting for him. The latter has found a long leather coat under Harmonica's saddle and they are identical to those used by McBain's murderers. Harmonica puts on the coat. It is too short for him. The sheriff is convinced of his innocence; Harmonica beats up the three tough guys and leaves.

An official of the bank in Flagstone shows Jill a certificate that McBain had entrusted to him fifteen years earlier: it is a deed to the Sweetwater property.

Harmonica and Cheyenne look admiringly at the facade of the station they have just finished constructiong.

*Jill (Claudia Cardinale), the heroine of the movie, with a
past as a prostitute and future as a businesswoman, in the
pursuit of memories.*

The auction scene is preceded by a long prologue in the barbershop where Frank is getting a shave. Silently, Harmonica observes the scene through the shop window. Leaning against the corner of a building he is whittling a piece of wood. He sees Jill arrive in a wagon with one of Frank's men; she turns to the sheriff to set the date of the auction of the Sweetwater property.

After the surprise intervention at the auction by Cheyenne and Harmonica, a man rushes to the barbershop to inform Frank who has just finished his shave.

Some scenes were originally longer than in the release version: Harmonica gets up again after the opening duel; the McBains return from the hunt just before the massacre; Harmonica tails Wobbles to Morton's private railway car. These scenes were put back into the edition restored in 1995 under the direction of Clavier Salizzato, with the assistance of Sergio Leone Production, Telepiù, Centro Sperimentale di Cinematografia Cineteca Nazionale. It is eleven minutes longer than the original.

* * *

"I don't want the government's money to go to *Once Upon a Time in the West*."
"And I don't want it to go to *Partner*."
These are the words of two Italian journalists (Mino Argentieri and Vinicio Marinucci) at a critics' conference in October, 1968. Old arguments. Art vs. industry, ivory tower vs. popularity, state-subsidized movies vs. American capital, molotov cocktails vs. Union Pacific... The reality is more complex. Bernardo Bertolucci, the director of *Partner,* had written the subject for *Once Upon a Time in the West.* The cultural fatherland of the two movies, appearances to the contrary, was neither Hanoi nor Washington, but Paris the (then) capital of movie-buffdom.

In 1968 politics and cinema went hand in hand. The youthful public went wild for *Bonnie and Clyde* which was anarchic and rétro at the same time, and committed directors were shooting movies that fell between left and pop: *Partner* (Dostoevsky meets Jerry Lewis); *Beneath the Sign of the Scorpion* by the Tavianis (Brecht meets the peplum); *Dillinger è morto* [Dillinger is dead] by Marco Ferreri (Marcuse meets Rauschenberg).

The Italian Western was running out of steam. From seventy-seven movies of the kind made in 1968, production had declined to thirty-one in 1969. Leone's last Western was

not so very Italian: Paramount was among the producers; in the cast figured three American stars of different schools (Henry Fonda, Jason Robards and Charles Bronson); locations were no longer only in Spain but also in Monument Valley, the very location where *Stagecoach* was shot.

Marshall McLuhan said that the subject of all Westerns was "Let's build a city." The game is even more fun when you are linking up the cities with stagecoaches, the telegraph and the railroads... Legendary companies lend their names to these movies: *Pony Express, Wells Fargo, Western Union, and Union Pacific.*

Leone too sings the epic of the first transcontinental railroads solemnly and with secret irony. He combines the Hollywood sterotypes with classical archetypes.

There is only one woman, a defenceless widow with a prostitute's past and a future as a businesswoman. In the West, one well knows, all social precedents are abolished and anybody can become somebody. Even a prostitute. The best female parts in Westerns are those of self-made women with an equivocal past who are ennobled more by economic independence than by nostalgia for their lost innocence (*Johnny Guitar* and *Rancho Notorious*). Even the legendary Scarlett O'Hara combines very dubious morals as regards men with a Calvinistic sense of business and an absolute worship of landed property. Leone's heroine is of the same breed, even if she has a more limited range of expressions (actually only two: amazement and diffidence). To make up for that she is full of dignity. She performs the simplest daily tasks, like warming up the coffee, drawing water from the well and distributing it to the workers, with all the solemnity of a vestal virgin.

The good hero, Harmonica, is even more primordial. He floats through the film like a ghost, talks in riddles, smiles sadly, is sparing in gesture and almost totally wordless. He prefers playing the mouth organ, always the same dirge-like tune, thus giving proof on more than one occasion of an impassiveness that is too perfect not to be hiding a deep, deep wound. In the end we learn that Harmonica only lives for vengeance: he is a tragic hero. His opposite, Cheyenne, the sage brigand, is always ready for a chat and never misses an opportunity to pontificate. Even when courting Jill, he does so with two-bit philosophy lessons and impertinent praise ("You remind me of my mother, the biggest slut in Alameda and the most on-the-ball woman whoever lived. Whoever was my father, for an hour or a month, was a lucky man.").

The two villains, in traditional style, do not trust each other

The beauty (Claudia Cardinale) and the indifferent (Charles Bronson).

and try to wipe each other out. There is a Western-type villain and a film *noir* type. Leone endows the former with a sinister grandeur by "wrong" casting as Hitchcock taught. Henry Fonda's calm presence and clear-eyed glance which have so often portrayed the Olympic serenity of the just man, here give a priestly gravity to the gestures of the evil character. Dressed perpetually in black, he is an elegant sadist who likes to humiliate his victims and see them groveling at his feet.

Morton, the other bad guy, is something halfway between a gangster and a tycoon. Visually, three things characterize him in almost comic-strip style: the chin strap and brass hand-rail he needs for support because he has tuberculosis of the bone, and the picture of the Pacific Ocean which is the goal of all his efforts. Even capitalists can be dreamers at times.

The five founding fathers Leone imagined are no less monumental and monolithic than the ones sculpted on Mount Rushmore. Their individual differences are less important than the gigantic quality they have in common, and in any case the moral differences of the good and the bad count for less than the historical gap between the two generations of pioneers: the nomadic adventure seekers and the new settlers determined to build something for themselves and hence more suited to the industrial civilization that is arising. This would all seem to take us back to Frederick J. Turner's theory of the frontier as a symbol of the perpetual rebirth of American society and to the autumnal Westerns that recount the extinction of the courageous breed of men (*Guns in the Afternoon* and *The Man Who Shot Liberty Valance*). We are at the very heart of the American tradition. However, while the heroes of Ford and Peckinpah become legendary even for their weaknesses (a drunken John Wayne who sets fire to the ranch, or a Randolph Scott who tries to escape with the loot from the bank), those of

The final showdown resembles a funeral rite and this 'operatic'
Western, hieratic and ironic, becomes a requiem mass for
the Western. Here, Henry Fonda and Charles Bronson.

Above: *Jill (Claudia Cardinale), as a generous woman.* **Left**: *Claudia Cardinale and Henry Fonda.*

Leone face their destinies with an inhuman dignity. One should not criticize certain librettos just because they lack psychological subtleties since, in the end, it will be up to the music to suggest these. And just that happens in certain scenes of *Once Upon a Time in the West* – for example, when Jill goes down to the station. Despite its being mostly filmed with outdoor shots, the air we breathe here is that of the opera house.

To emphasize the vastness of his stage, Leone omits presenting any supporting characters and never allows his five heroes to appear all at once (in three hours of projection time, Cheyenne never meets Frank, and Jill never meets Morton).

The love of ruins. Claudio Mancini, Dino Mele and Henry Fonda.

Nothing could be further from the narrative functionalism of the American Western. Here the length of the scenes is not proportional to their story interest but rather to their liturgical content. Leone's favorite rites seem to be the waiting and the agony. In the prologue three shady characters await the arrival of the train. To kill time, the first patiently maneuvers a pesky fly into the barrel of his gun, the second submits, motionless, to the slow dripping of water from the ceiling into his hat and then drinks it, while the third cracks his knuckles. It is a quote from *High Noon*. Deprived of all suspense (we have no idea who is arriving) it becomes a classic stereotype in an almost pure state, an ironical homage to the proverbial patience of the Westerner.

Long waiting again occurs during Jill's first night at the ranch where she is baptized into the immense solitude of the West; typical is the scene on the bed, culminating in a frame à la von Sternberg, in which she is seen through the bed's lace canopy, looking like a frightened queen.

To obtain such mythological emphasis, Leone is capable of sacrificing some spectacular effects. For example, he does not shoot the gunfight on the train where Morton and Cheyenne are killed. Instead he dwells at length on their final agony. Morton dies beside his train, creeping with pathetic tenacity towards a pool which the soughing of waves in the sound-track transforms into a surrogate for that ocean the tycoon never managed to reach. Cheyenne dies as composed as a samurai: he drops to the ground and asks his companion to move off.

Just as ritualistic are the exchanges of threats. Each time it seems that the characters are about to attack each other, but then nothing happens. Cheyenne does not draw his Colt, Jill does not grab the kitchen knife and Morton closes the drawer where he keeps his pistol. They all give great proofs of self control. But too many false alarms are an invitation to smirk.

These exchanges of threats remind us of the swaggering nature of the heroes of the dollar trilogy here wrapped in a vague veil of mystery. Leone, no less swaggering and mysterious than his characters, is a master in the art of keeping one waiting and reveals the avenger's motives in flashback, and only at the exact moment of his vengeance, which takes on an almost sacred, ritual tone.

Here is the operatic Western, hieratic and ironic, which becomes a requiem mass for the Western genre itself.

Admittedly there is no lack of crowd-pleasing scenes: two prolix gunfights (on the train and in the streets of Flagstone) made vivid by some optical illusions and a sex scene dominated by Henry Fonda's half-cynical, half-bitter words. Here, as in other scenes of the movie, everything is more acted, evoked, than directly lived.

The effect is enhanced by the rather unreal quality of space, where the desert suggests that everything is temporary. Even the images of labor and of progress partake of the spectral. In *My Darling Clementine* the whole town danced on the foundations of the church under construction, announcing a radiant future. Here, it is Cheyenne's brigands who measure the ground and sink the piles on which the station will be erected. And they do it only out of gallantry towards Jill. The city being built looks like a phantom city, or perhaps merely a toy city immersed in a deceiving light which slightly alters its proportions to the scale of that model of the station that Jill finds when rummaging in the drawers in a scene shot with an intimate, almost crepuscular flavor. Even the cruelest, episode of the whole picture, the lynching at the stone arch, seems to come from some ancient oriental story. Leone has kept the ambitious promise made in the title: to make us continually feel the "once upon a time."

Curiously, two movies linked to the legendary past and the science-fiction future, full of nostalgia for the epic and of skepticism regarding the future of humanity, were to become the main cult movies of 1968: *Once Upon a Time in the West* and *2001: A Space Odyssey*.

Duck! You Sucker

A quotation from Mao: "The Revolution is no gala lunch..." As the opening titles are shown, a peon, Juan (Rod Steiger) urinates against a tree and then flags down a stagecoach along a country road. The guards search him carefully, make him pay his passage and let him into the coach.

Inside the sumptuously furnished vehicle, the passengers (a clergyman, an elegant lady, an American...) are eating lunch. To humiliate Juan they make him sit on a foot stool and chat derisively about the promiscuous ways of the peasants.

The stagecoach has to slow down. Some peons slip under the vehicle, block the wheels and massacre the guards in a shoot-out. They are Juan's sons, his old father and some of his men.

One passenger, who tries to get out his pistol, is killed. The woman is dragged by Juan behind the house where in a rather still and passive way she lets him rape her. All the passengers are robbed of their valuables and clothes and are boarded onto a wagon which is pushed downhill and ends up in a watering hole.

Now Juan and his family are traveling in the stagecoach. They stop suddenly because of a landslide brought on by an explosion. It is the work of Sean (James Coburn), an Irish terrorist who is practicing the use of dynamite. He is traveling on a motorcycle and his overalls are lined with explosives. The two now embark on a loud exchange of insults. The Mexican shoots out a tire of Sean's motorcycle. The latter, in turn, rips open the roof of the coach with nitroglycerin. After giving them another taste of explosives, he gets them to repair his tire. One of Juan's men tries to use the dynamite by himself but he gets the wrong fuse and is blown up.

The two of them have an outdoor lunch on the elegant seats removed from the stagecoach. Sean lets his mind dwell on memories. Flashback. An automobile excursion in the Irish countryside. In the car Sean, a friend, and a girl. Sean and the girl kiss.

Juan had other things on his mind and proposes an alliance to rob the famous Mesa Verde bank. Sean declines and goes off on his motorcycle. The irate Mexican shoots a hole in his gas tank, and Sean, in turn, blows up the coach. Then he goes off on foot towards a mine where he has been engaged to search for veins of silver.

One night Sean, who happens to find himself near an old,

abandoned mission, mistakes some shadows moving among the ruins for Juan and his men. He sets up mines around the area and is preparing to explode them when Juan appears and presses the detonator with his foot. Inside the fort were the mine owner and some soldiers whom Juan had lured to the spot. Sean, now without a job and with the law on his trail, is obliged to join up with the brigands.

The gang is riding alongside the railroad tracks when a train

Duck! You Sucker.
Italian poster.

83

Juan speaks with God, like Don Camillo, and loves his family.

separates Sean from the Mexicans for a few minutes. Sean seizes the opportunity to escape.

Juan and his sons are riding on a train at night. With them in the compartment is Dr. Villega (Romolo Valli) immersed in a book. A policeman is on the point of recognizing Juan, who stabs him and throws him off the train. Another policeman intervenes and Juan holds up his hands, but very soon the policeman must surrender when Dr. Villega points a pistol to his back. Thus the bandit throws the second guard from the train too.

The group gets off at the Mesa Verde station. The streets are full of soldiers. From the announcements put up all over town, the benevolent governor declares he offers bread and justice.

A man who is trying to escape from the soldiers runs towards Juan and, struck by a bullet in the back, dies in his arms. Next, the bandit happens to witness the execution of three political prisoners. Finally, he meets Sean in a tavern facing the bank.

Flashback. Sean's Irish friend is handing out a revolutionary newspaper in a Dublin pub. Return to the present. John leads the Mexican into the cellar of an inn which serves as a hideout for the conspirators. Villega is finishing up attending to one of them and he reveals the plan for a general rebellion: Juan is to hold up the bank. The rogue is happy to accept the job since he is counting on making off with the loot.

On the day of the insurrection, Sean, installed in the tavern, blows up the entrance door of the bank with a charge of dynamite hidden in the toy train that one of Juan's sons has dragged down under the building. The Mexican leads his men into the bank, but in the safes, instead of gold, he finds dozens of political prisoners who acclaim him a hero of the revolution. This does not seem to console him for the loss of the booty.

In a desert area, Gunther Reza, the Teutonic condottiere of Huerta's troops, is traveling in an armored car at the head of some marching soldiers.

Sean and Juan are resting in the rebel's camp. The Mexican rants bitterly and resentfully about the futility of all revolutions.

The rebels shake off their pursuers by doubling back towards the grotto of San Isidro. Sean and Juan, for their part, are lying in wait for the enemy troops from the heights of a hill overlooking a bridge. The Irishman kills time by napping while the Mexican seethes with anger over such a display of phlegm. As soon as Huerta's troops are on the bridge, the two begin to machine-gun them until they take cover under the arcades. Then Sean stops shooting, puts cotton into his ears and, activating the detonator, blows up the bridge. Gunther Reza comes out of it uninjured.

In the San Isidro grotto, Juan, seized by desperation, rips a chain with a crucifix from his neck and, throwing all caution to the winds, grabs a machine gun and goes out to confront the

soldiers who quickly take him prisoner. In the meantine Sean discovers the bodies of the massacred rebels. Among them are the Mexican's father and all his sons.

At night, in a courtyard hammered by rain and lit by the lights of military trucks, several conspirators are executed after first having to pass before Gunther Reza's truck. Beside him Dr. Villega is sitting, his faced marked with bruises, and identifies the prisoners. Among the small crowd witnessing the scene is Sean who recognizes Villega and recalls a similar occurrence in a Dublin pub.

Flashback. The English police smash their way into a pub and Sean's friend, his face swollen by thrashing, identifies some of the customers. When Sean's turn comes, he turns and shoots with a gun hidden in a newspaper.

Return to the present. The condemned fall under the hail of bullets. An officer gives them the *coup de grace* with his pistol.

The next day Juan is about to face the firing squad in the courtyard of a barracks when the Irishman attacks the platoon with dynamite and escapes on his motorcycle taking the condemned man with him.

Near the railroad a mass execution of political prisoners is taking place. By now Huerta's defeat is judged to be imminent and at the station a great throng is waiting for the train to the United States. But not all of them manage to board it. An officer who has hidden his uniform under an overcoat is shot down together with two prisoners. Juan and Sean, hidden in the cattle car, are looking forward to grandiose hold-ups in the land of the dollar. The last to board is the governor, the one with his picture on all the posters.

As Sean is strangling a wild rooster that is disturbing his sleep by fluttering its wings, a truck on the tracks brings the train to a halt. The rebels begin their assault. The governor tries to flee, enters the cattle car and is captured by John and Juan. The images of his massacred family come into Juan's mind, but when the governor offers him a bag full of valuables in exchange for his life, he stares at the contents and seems tempted. The governor takes advantage of his distraction to open the doors of the car and only then does Juan decide to kill him with two bullets in the back. He wants to reach the border with the loot, but the rebels who have won the day, acclaim him as a hero and carry him around in triumph.

On the moving train, in the car being used by the rebels as a general headquarters, they are thinking about how to block a train Huerta has sent after them. Sean proposes dynamite. To put his plan into action he only needs one man, Dr. Villega.

Gunther Reza is brushing his teeth on the military train. It is night. Villega, alone with Sean on the moving locomotive, realizes that the other knows of his betrayal and asks his pardon.

The Irishman remembers (in flashback) the end of the episode in the pub where he killed not only the policemen but his own friend who had given in to torture.

That act must have cost him a lot and now he declines to inflict the same punishment on the doctor. The locomotive, loaded with dynamite, proceeds towards the military train. Sean lights the fuse and leaps off. Villega decides to redeem himself with a heroic death. The trains collide and blow up. The rebels, hidden behind the irrigators, unleash their attack on the survivors. Sean is hit in the back by Gunther Reza. For vengeance Juan mows him down with his machine gun then vents his fury by blasting away at the corpse. As the Irishman dies, he prophesies that Juan will be named a general and gives him back the chain with the crucifix. Then, as Juan goes off in search of help, he takes his cigar and ignites the arsenal he carries on his person. As the end credits unroll we see Juan's distraught face, "And now what becomes of me?"

Principal scenes cut from the Italian release version

At first, Sean and Juan's trip in the desert was much longer. (At a certain point, the boys take the Irishman's motorcycle and completely dismantle it; the father yells at them, and they have to put it back together.)

After their victorious battle on the bridge, the rebels reunite in the grottoes. They look worried. In flashback, Sean recalls his past in Ireland. Overcome with rage he throws a bottle at a gramophone.

Dr. Villega is tortured by Gunther Reza and his men. Only their shadows on the wall are visible.

The epilogue: A flashback with a long panorama of the great green spaces of Ireland. Sean kisses a girl under a tree. So does his friend, without John seeming to be jealous. This scene, that lasts three minutes and forty seconds was uncut from versions in other European countries and was put back into the 1996 version, restored under the direction of Claver Salizzato, with the aid of Sergio Leone Production, Telepiù, and Centro Sperimentale di Cinematografia Cineteca Nazionale.

* * *

In 1971 the latest box-office miracle is Dario Argento's *The Bird With the Crystal Plumage* which inaugurates a new genre, the Italian thriller. The recipe is not much different from that of the Western: multiply the number of homicides, insist on truculence, expand the suspense with music, create an unusual look (American actors in a glass and cement Italy). It is the film *noir* of the age of distraction which involves no one emotionally and which can be followed intermittently like television and which flatters the viewer who feels erudite when he manages to recognize mechanisms and quotations. Argento, though less gifted than Leone, will have a similar destiny: once the detective story scheme of the first films is abolished, he will devote himself to a kind of delirious mysticism of terror (*Suspiria, Inferno* and *Tenebre* [Darkness]).

There are already some who propose a return to the private, to sentiment. It is the year of *Love Story* and a lucky Italian melodrama *The Anonymus Venetian* by Enrico Maria Salerno with Tony Musante, condemned by an incurable malady, who tries to win back his wife, Florinda Bolkan, in the setting of a putrefying Venice.

Cultural trend continued to demand serious commitment. There was the commitment of directors such as Montaldo and Damiano Damiani to the justice thriller and with positive heroes (*Sacco and Vanzetti, Confessions of a Police Captain*). And then there was the more sophisticated commitment of Elio Petri (*Investigation of a Citizen Above Suspicion*) with the police commissioner's delusions of grandeur and *La classe operaia va in paradiso* [The working class goes to paradise], with its workers' nightmares of grandeur, both of them entrusted to Gian Maria Volonté's grotesque actor's mask. But the secondary characters are a shade too wise (and stereotyped) while the dialogues sound like pamphlets. Behind the delirium one smells the committee room.

Even certain master directors seem to be infected with the radical and apocalyptic spirit of these times. Visconti shoots *The Damned* about the relationship between Nazism and heavy industry with echoes of Thomas Mann, Shakespeare, Dostoevsky and Wagner, all of them subsumed under a levelling moralizing that diminishes the "chiaroscuro" definition of his anti-heroes. In *Zabriskie Point* Antonioni applied his "surface-of-the-world style" to the campus students whom he portrayed as rebellious angels trying to share their most audacious dreams. The happy ending shows refrigerators, television sets and other symbols of the consumer society exploding in slow motion.

Even the directors of Westerns discover the revolution, the Mexican one, that was suited to combine spectacle and ideology because of the way it mixed brigandage and class struggle. And yet, despite some interesting subjects by Donati or Solinas (*Face to Face* and *A Bullet for the General*) the films mix the over-ambitious and the sophomoric.

Thomas Milian plays the eccentric rebel peon by wearing a Che Guevara beret; Volonté as a Mexican bandit speaks half Italian, half Spanish and sneers all the time; Franco Nero illustrates the idea behind revolution to Tony Musante with a

The Irishman (James Coburn), is the master when it comes to arms and morals; the Mexican (Rod Steiger) is a rebellious and ridiculous disciple, with his combination of wild instinct, peasant simplicity and religious faith.

*Some of the most spectacular scenes have an almost
funereal solemnity.*

parable, using a naked woman ("Keep in mind that the rich are the head, the ones who command and make all the others work; while the poor are the backside, the lower half..."); Mark Damon asks himself between tortures and shoot-outs if it is the southern slaves or the northern workers who are most exploited; and a Yankee capitalist threatens: "I don't like people touching my capital." These Westerns seem to be bad copies of political revolutionary films that never saw the light.

The subject of Sergio Corbucci's *(A Professional Gun)*, transferred from Mexico to the Antilles, served as a point of departure for Gillo Pontecorvo's *Queimada* (also known as *Burn!*), a chilling lesson on neo-colonialism offered by a sluggish Marlon Brando. But perhaps the true, noble father of third-world Westerns is a director himself of the third world: Glauber Rocha, the creator of *Antonio das mortes*, a barbarous ballad about a kind of Brazilian bounty hunter.

However sensitive Leone may have been to social commitment (he participated in a film of "counter-information" on the Piazza Fontana bombing entitled *12 dicembre*), he seems not to have been interested in shooting a populist Western. He limited himself to writing a script for his assistant Giancarlo Santi and arranging for the production. But Rod Steiger and James Coburn insisted on being directed by the master himself. And this climate of improvisation may have been salubrious. Leone felt no obligation to direct an auteur film, but only to make a solid movie using a subject that had already been handled other times, somewhat in the way that American directors do.

It has always been a prerogative of a spectacular epic to mix the sacred and the profane, and in 1971 there was nothing more sacred than revolution. *Duck! You Sucker* juxtaposes in the most nonchalant way quotations from Mao Tse Tung with bridges that are blown up (as in *For Whom the Bell Tolls*); homage to the IRA, and *Saratoga Trunk*-type locomotive collisions.

But Leone has the good taste not to take himself altogether seriously. His heroes are comic-book style supermen. The Irishman, a professional revolutionary, travels on a motorcycle and wears overalls lined with explosives. At the end, wounded in the back, he kills himself by blowing up the arsenal he carries on him, like a magician or like 'Pierrot le fou' (there is also a precedent in Ford's *Three Bad Men*). The Mexican is a histrionic and rough bandit (the movie opens with a detailed shot of him urinating). The villain is a Prussian, a warlord, who travels in an armored car, drinks raw eggs for breakfast and, even on the train, does not forget to brush his teeth. Perhaps he is a shade immortal, to judge by the way he survives the bridge

The villain, Colonel Gunther Reza (Domingo Antoine), is a warlord who travels in a German-made tank.

James Coburn, the explosive Irishman.

massacre unharmed wearing an irate expression that is a promise of reprisals in the next episode. There is also a traitor, a doctor who cannot stand up to torture. But he redeems himself with a heroic sacrifice.

In short, everything must turn out larger than life, but this does not happen all the time. For example, the friendship between the two heroes, carbon copies of those by now standard figures in the political Western, the gringo and the peon, is portrayed in the most predictable paternalistic way. (From this point of view *A Bullet for the General* was more

interesting, where the peon, disgusted by the gringo's cynicism, ends up killing him.)

The Irishman is the teacher, with regard to firearms as well as morality; the Mexican a recalcitrant disciple in whom dwell ferocious instincts, peasant simplicity, and religious faith. Juan speaks with God, like Don Camillo, and loves his family: he converts to the revolution above all to avenge his children. (Here there is an allusion to the Italian Resistance: Alcide Cervi and his seven children killed by the Nazis.) He is not even particularly violent. In the end, when he takes the governor prisoner, he seriously hesitates before killing him; and he makes the decision to do it only after considering all his crimes and after he tries to escape. Before he dies, the Irishman gives him back the crucifix that Juan had thrown away in a moment of despair over the death of his sons. An edifying ending which counterbalances the relative irreverence of the beginning, in Buñuel style, where the Mexican robs and strips the passengers in a luxury stagecoach; representatives of the backbone of society, a priest included. In the foreign edition and the restored one, the ending is followed by a relatively libertarian, Lelouch-style epilogue in which the two Irish conspirators kiss the same girl in slow motion under the branches of a tree.

But where Leone's populist, picaresque taste finds original accents is in the Chaplin-inspired bank hold-up where Juan and his men open the safe and instead of money find dozens of half-starved political prisoners. And his mannerist and melodramatic spirit return to splendor in the betrayal episode in which some have seen the spirit of Borges. Leone does things in a big way, he shows us almost simultaneously two betrayals (obtained under torture) in two different revolutions, the Mexican and the Irish. A flashback lasting barely a minute is enough for him to suspend narrative time and suggest a metaphysics of betrayal.

Leone's originality is also revealed by the fact that whereas in the Westerns of Damiani, Sollima and Corbucci entrusted the revolutionary message to dialogue much more than to action scenes – terribly approximate and unconvincing – in Leone, it is more or less quite the opposite that happens. The relations between the leads are treated in a comically heroic style (duels, ritual threats, demonstrations of pyrotechnical skill...), while the spectacular scenes have an almost funereal gravity that was appreciated even by a critic hostile to Westerns like Alberto Moravia. Mostly they are execution scenes where the hero, not being able to come to the aid of the condemned, watches the firing squad from a hiding place, and so they seem more authentic and inevitable. This tragic voyeurism is enhanced in the night-time execution, where the traitor identifies the prisoners who are being executed and the Irishman, hidden among the crowd, recognizes the traitor in turn. The night, the rain, the courtyard lit by the headlights of the trucks, the stripes of white paint on the walls, all accentuate the atmosphere of mourning. When the Huerta regime vacillates, a movement of the helicopter crane reveals an apocalyptic scene: dozens of political prisoners massed in parallel trenches hurriedly being shot by soldiers stationed upon the parapets. (For once Leone does not take his time, shoots no close-ups, but makes one long

take and the effect is even stronger – as if one were passing there by chance.)

A pity that Leone does not also tell us of the revolutionary terror; but, after all, his film is merely a spectacular where one has to be able to distinguish the good from the bad. Furthermore even an auteur epic such as *1900* is no less schematic with its De Amicis-style stereotypes (vigorous proletarians, intrepid little school mistresses, heartless bosses) brought up to date with sex and scenes straight out of the Grand Guignol.

And, in general, it is no longer so easy to distinguish between high-brow or low-brow films. How, for example, does one classify Dario Argento's *Le cinque giornate* [The five days] that narrates the Risorgimento in cynical anti-rhetorical cabaret terms? Not to mention certain rickety black comedies by Lina Wertmüller such as *The Seduction of Mimi* that drip with folklore, ethnic clichés, and bad taste, but which at least do not hide social conflicts.

At times even the usual protagonists of typical Italian comedy visit the real life of the present. In Dino Risi's *Mordi e fuggi* [Bite and run], the industrialist Mastroianni is kidnapped by terrorists and makes every compromise to save his neck. In Monicelli's *A Very Little Man*, Alberto Sordi as an office worker takes revenge for the death of his son during a hold-up by kidnapping and meticulously torturing the murderer. Even when he is acting in a vile or sadistic way, the eternal champion of the art-of-getting-by is still the most likeable and vital character since in such films the powers that be are only caricatures and the young are a hostile and incomprehensible race.

Even "Z" movies are on the side of the silent majority, but without humor. The model is Michael Winner's *Death Wish*. Usually there is a hero fed up with the slowness of the legal process who decides to take the law into his own hands and resorts to massacres worthy of the early Italian Westerns.

On the other hand, the few Westerns produced these days are pretentious and extravagant like Lucio Fulci's *I quattro dell'Apocalisse* [The apocalypse four] which combines Bret Harte's outcasts with the peyote of Castaneda and Corbucci's sadism; or else they are frankly burlesques like the Trinity series with Bud Spencer and Terence Hill, where the Western has by now been reduced to a local-color level to the point that the pair can transform themselves into pirates or cops in other movies. Their most original characteristic is a kind of violence that is both exaggerated and innocuous as in cartoons even while being a little monotonous.

Leone, too, in the thirteen years that separate *Duck! You*

Sucker from *Once Upon a Time in America,* besides directing some TV commercials, produced two Westerns starring Terence Hill for the Rafran Cinematografica (the name taken from the initials of his three children: Raffaella, born in 1961; Francesca, born in 1964; and Andrea, born in 1968).

My Name Is Nobody by Tonino Valerii is at once a homage to and a parody of Leone's baroque style, with shoot-outs taking place in mirrored labyrinths, its wild bunch charging to the music of *The Ride of the Valkyries,* and Henry Fonda confronting 150 adversaries single-handedly, hoping to go down in history books. His wish is immediately granted. With the magic of editing, every now and then a gunfight freezes into a still shot and ends up printed in the pages of a book. Irony towards mythology, always an undercurrent in Leone, is here made explicit.

Less successful, Damiano Damiani's *A Genius* is a farce where clergymen preach in brothels, the military are completely corrupt and pistols come out of their holsters and shoot by themselves. The one refreshing note is Miou Miou's emancipated smile.

For a couple of years, while the series that opened with *A Fistful of Dollars* was beginning to run out of steam, one had begun to catch glimpses of its influence in American Westerns, at least in the cruelty of certain scenes and perhaps in a certain desecrating spirit. Already in 1968, for example, there had been the interesting *Hang'em High* by Ted Post (the direction had

first been offered to Leone), a nocturnal and Lang-like movie where the legal hangings of the guilty are no less frightful than the lynchings of innocents and where there is nothing exalting in the vengeance, even if the avenger is Clint Eastwood. And the following year in *The Wild Bunch,* Peckinpah had recounted with stubborn pessimism (and occasionally sincere feeling) the end of adventurous ideals, celebrating the only remaining form of heroism in the nihilistic violence of the finale.

And again, twenty years after *Duck! You Sucker,* two directors of the uncertain Western revival express their debt to Leone.

If Sam Raimi in *The Quick and the Dead,* the bloody chronicle of a direct-elimination tournament between gunmen, revives the taste for the macabre pastiche that was typical of the Spaghetti Western, so Clint Eastwood in *The Unforgiven* (dedicated "to Sergio and Don"), the story of vengeance on commission narrated in a terribly unadorned style, succeeds in overcoming both Puritan moralizing and Italian cynicism. Just as the heroes no longer have such perfect aim, so justice proceeds by inevitable and bloody approximations, and not even the dividing line between good and bad is very clear anymore (even though everyone still fools themselves into thinking they see it). Not even Leone with his funereal skepticism had reached such a degree of lucidity. He had always still believed in the game of heroism a little.

Before the explosion (**opposite page**) *and after the execution.*

There is only the past seen by the future, or the future seen by the past, memory that blends with pure fantasy. Robert De Niro crossing the threshold of time.

Once Upon a Time in America

1984

[A Chinese shadow play that represents the eternal struggle between good and evil. At the side of the screen, drum, bell and gamelan players. In the theater only a few sleepy spectators.]

Opening titles against a black background. Out of the silence arises the song *God Bless America*.

New York, 1933. A young lady, Eve (Darlanne Fleugel), returns to her room where she is attacked by three gangsters. They want to know where Noodles is hiding. She won't talk. They kill her with two pistol shots.

Fat Moe, the obese proprietor of the bar that bears his name, is beaten up in his bar by the girl's killers and ends up by talking: Noodles is at the Chinese theater.

In an opium den above the theater, Noodles (Robert De Niro) is in an opium trance. He reads in a newspaper that three whisky smugglers have just been shot by the police.

Flashback (punctuated with twenty-two rings of the telephone). The site of the massacre at dawn. A burnt truck, the cargo of whisky spilled out, the police who are covering the corpses of the three gangsters, Patsy, Cockeye and Max (the last with his face burnt beyond recognition); Noodles among the crowd observing the scene; the night before during a goodbye party to Prohibition in the speakeasy below Fat Moe's, Noodles who telephones to the police.

Return to the present. Two of the girl's killers enter the theater looking for Noodles among the audience of a Chinese shadow play. But he manages just in time to vanish and reach Fat Moe's. Here, by an ingenious maneuver, he eliminates the one killer who has stayed on guard duty and he has the bar owner give him a key.

In a railway station Noodles opens a locker containing a suitcase. Probably he was expecting it to be full of money and instead he only finds old newspaper. He buys a one-way ticket to any destination at all.

The same station in 1968. Noodles, sixty years old, has just arrived and rents a car.

After stopping near a Jewish cemetery being demolished he goes to visit his old friend Fat Moe at his bar and shows him an anonymous letter he has just received. Someone has discovered where he has been hiding out for thirty-five years. The two friends cannot understand who could have taken the million dollars that represented the gang's joint fund. Noodles, excited by memories, makes the rounds of the bar, looks at the yellowed photographs of his friends, goes into the toilet that has a vent opening on the warehouse.

1922. From that same vent the fourteen-year-old Noodles is spying on the beautiful Deborah, a girl of his own age and Fat Moe's sister, who is dancing to the tune of "Amapola" played on a gramophone. Even though she knows he is looking, Deborah nonchalantly changes clothes and goes off to her dancing lesson.

Noodles catches her up in the street, but the haughty girl snubs him. He meets his gang mates, Cockeye, Patsy and Dominic who have been given the job of extorting from a newspaper. The four of them, carrying a pump, spray the newsstand with gasoline and set it on fire.

They are rewarded by Monkey, proprietor of a speakeasy, who lets them chose a customer of his to rip off. The boys eye a valuable watch sticking out of the pocket of a drunk. They follow him into the street but, as they are about to attack him, a wagon loaded with household goods passes and blond Max jumps down, lifts the man onto the wagon and gives him a ride. The neighborhood cop chases the kids away brusquely.

When Noodles gets home he holes up in the toilet to read *Martin Eden*. Peggy, a curvaceous and provocative young girl, joins him there. They joke and touch each other, but if he wants her she demands a charlotte russe with whipped cream. Noodles leaves her in possession of the toilet.

In the street he meets Max who is moving with his family. Noodles waits until he is busy unloading a chandelier to steal the drunk's watch from him. The same cop turns up and seizes the stolen watch.

At dawn the four delinquents, joined by Max, attack a black trumpet player and rob him of his trumpet and wallet. Max decides that they are not going to work for others anymore.

Patsy, who has bought a charlotte russe to pay Peggy with, cannot resist his own greediness and devours it in an instant as he is waiting for the girl on the stairs. As a result he has to be satisfied with spying on her when she meets the neighborhood cop on a roof terrace. The friends, who are quickly informed of what is happening, photograph the couple in a compromising position and blackmail the policeman: besides giving them back the watch he must no longer protect Bugsy, the little boss of the neighborhood, and must allow Max and Noodles to enjoy Peggy's charms free of charge. They do so at once.

Darlanne Fleugel in a scene cut from the release version of the film.

On one Passover day, when everyone is at the synagogue, Noodles and Deborah kiss in the back room of Fat Moe's place. Then, when Max and Noodles are in the courtyard, Bugsy and his gang arrive. Max and Noodles, guilty of working on their own, are beaten up savagely. When Noodles, bleeding, knocks on her door, Deborah does not open to him.

In the clandestine distillery of the Capuano brothers, Noodles presents a system he has thought up for salvaging the whisky that the bootleggers habitually are forced to dump into the sea when the police boats arrive. It is a question of filling sacks with salt that break after a few hours underwater and let the cargo tied to buoys come to the surface. Noodles tries it out in a barrel.

The invention works even when it is repeated in the bay. The boys are enthusiastic – they will get ten per cent of every salvaged cargo.

At the train station, the five boys, dressed up in new clothes, put the suitcase containing the gang's joint fund in a locker and solemnly swear fidelity. The key to the locker is entrusted to Fat Moe.

Outside the station they run into Bugsy who pursues them in a rage (in a scene that was not shot, Bugsy is arrested while Max and Noodles deride him from a distance) and he shoots little Dominic. In self defence, Noodles plants a knife in his adversary's stomach, then, in a panic, also hits a policeman who comes to break up the brawl. A second policeman stuns him with his truncheon.

The police van, with Noodles inside, enters the prison. From far off his three friends wave goodbye to him.

1968. Noodles enters the chapel of the cemetery where his three friends are buried. Automatically a tape begins playing a march that Cockeye used to play on his flute to accompany the gang's activities. A small key hangs from a tablet.

[The woman director of the cemetery appears and says that she does not know who had this tomb built. In the street Noodles has the impression that a black limousine is following him and he writes down the license number.]

In the train station Noodles uses the key taken from the tomb to open a locker. There he finds a suitcase full of banknotes and a written note: "This is in payment of your next contract." While he is walking cautiously under an elevated road, a frisbee flies over his head.

1932. After having spent nine years in prison, Noodles is released and finds Max (James Woods) waiting for him at the wheel of an undertaker's van. Inside there is the pretended corpse of a gaudy redhead who comes to life and pulls Noodles in with an inviting air. In a clandestine tavern in Fat Moe's basement, Patsy, Cockeye and Fat Moe are celebrating the convict's release. Also there are Peggy, who has become a high-class prostitute, and Deborah (Elizabeth McGovern) who has become a successful ballerina. The boys go up to the second floor where, during a lunch, Noodles is presented to the boss Frankie and to Joe who has asked for some men to pull off a jewelry heist in Detroit.

The hold-up takes place. The terrified owner hands over the diamonds held in the safe while Carol (Tuesday Weld), the secretary who is an accomplice of the gangsters, becomes hysterical and incites Noodles to beat and rape her.

On the outskirts of Detroit the bandits deliver the diamonds to Joe, get their money, and then kill Joe and his men. A survivor tries to hide in a nearby factory in a washing machine. Noodles finds him and eliminates him. On the way back in the car, Noodles, irritated with Max about the bloody end to the affair, presses the accelerator and plunges the car into the lake.

[Everyone except Noodles emerges immediately...]

1968. [Near Senator Bailey's villa where a mysterious garbage truck is parked, Noodles sees the black limousine again, which blows up with an enormous blast.]

A television broadcast shows how the remains of the car are salvaged in the course of an investigation on Senator Bailey who has been accused of corruption. Seated in Fat Moe's bar, Noodles happens to see the program and recognizes Jimmy Conway among the people interviewed, the old Truckers' Union president.

1932. In a deserted slaughter house, Jimmy, then a young union man has gasoline poured over him by two gangsters who threaten to make him into a human torch if he does not call off a strike. Noodles and his men arrive, having taken Crowning hostage, the boss of the truck owners' organization. The two gangs exchange prisoners.

Coming out of a hospital, Aiello, the chief of police, talks jokingly with reporters. He is on cloud nine because after four daughters his wife has finally given birth to a boy.

Dressed as doctors, Noodles and his men get into the hospital nursery, where they change identification tags for all the newborn babies, having first made a note of the real identity numbers.

In his wife's room, Aiello discovers that *his* baby is a girl. At that very moment a phone call arrives from Noodles: if he wants his son back, Aiello must call the police out of the factory where scabs have replaced the striking workers. But Patsy has lost the

numbers indicating the identities of the newborn babies, so Aiello is given one at random.

Noodles has telephoned from a cathouse where he recognizes one of the girls as Carol, the secretary-accomplice of the Detroit hold-up. The four friends think up a joking way of getting her to recognize them: they cover their faces with handkerchiefs and unbutton their pants.

[While waiting for Deborah at the stage door of a Broadway theater, Noodles has a bitter exchange of repartee with his chauffeur, a Jew escaped from Germany.]

Noodles has dinner with Deborah in a seaside restaurant. The two dance in a romantic atmosphere. On the beach he tells her that he had constantly thought about her during his long years of prison and asks her to be his woman. But Deborah is consumed by her career and tells him that she is leaving for Hollywood the next day. Later, in the car, Noodles misunderstands her affectionate behavior and gives vent to his disappointment by raping her.

[At Fat Moe's, Noodles tries to drown his guilt feelings in alcohol. He picks up a young hooker, Eve, but in the bedroom he immediately falls asleep.]

[The next day Noodles catches a glimpse of Deborah seated at a table in the station restaurant and he follows her along the track.]

The majesty of the trivial. Beneath a sumptuous ceiling, Carol (Tuesday Weld) is raped by Noodles (Robert De Niro).

The different stages of life. Above: *Jennifer Connelly, Scott Tiler (Deborah and Noodles as teenagers), Elizabeth McGovern, James Woods (Max). Opposite page: Robert De Niro (Noodles) young and old, and an aged James Woods.*

The train leaves and Deborah pulls down the shade of her carriage window, thus excluding him definitively from her life.

At a meeting of the gang in Fat Moe's office, Noodles meets Max, more overbearing and megalomaniac than ever, in the company of Carol, who has become his girl. The phone rings. It is Jimmy calling from a public phone booth and an instant later he is gunned down by the machine guns of his rivals' killers.

Coming out of the Plaza, Crowning's two bodyguards are killed by Max and Noodles hiding in a wardrobe. Crowning is terrified.

In a hospital room, Jimmy, with a wounded leg, celebrates

the union's victory, primarily due to the activities of the gangsters. A politician is present who proposes that the boys enter the business world. Max is agreeable, Noodles not.

Noodles and Max, together with Carol and Eve, are enjoying themselves on the beach at Miami. They read in the newspapers of the imminent end of Prohibition. They are out of work but have a million dollars. To end their career with a bang, Max proposes a hold up at the Federal Reserve Bank of Manhattan. Noodles tells him he is crazy and Max punches him for it.

[1968. Carol, living in a retirement home, tells Noodles that Max was about to go insane like his father.]

1933. In a car, Carol and Noodles plan to squeal on Max to keep him from the absurd attempt of holding up the Federal Reserve Bank and bringing about a pointless massacre.

While the end of Prohibition is being celebrated at Fat Moe's, Noodles phones the police to inform them that the gangsters are about to escort a last load of bootleg whisky. He is expecting them all to be arrested, himself included, but it is the only way to foil Max's crazy plan. The latter dispenses him from going with the escort, and when Noodles calls him crazy he goes into a rage and stuns him with the butt of his pistol.

1968. At the retirement home Carol tells Noodles that Max did not want to end up in an insane asylum, so he himself planted the idea in his friends' heads of denouncing him and when the police stopped the truck he was the one who opened fire.

[In a theater, Deborah is playing the death of Cleopatra. Sitting in the audience, Noodles watches her.]

In her dressing room, while she is taking off her make-up, Noodles asks her if he should accept the mysterious invitation to Senator Bailey's party, Deborah's companion of many years. She tries to discourage him from going so as not to ruin the memories of their youth. As he leaves the dressing room, Noodles runs into Senator Bailey's son who is the spitting image of Max as an adolescent.

On the night of the party the villa is crowded with guests. [In one room, Jimmy is talking to Senator Bailey who is none other than Max resuscitated. He tries to convince him to kill himself to prevent an investigating committee from bringing their past to light.]

Max, now alone, receives Noodles. The old Senator's invitation has a precise purpose: seeing that he must die, he wants it to be by the hand of his old friend. Bailey owes him a big debt: he took his money and his woman and left him to bear the remorse for all those years. Of course, the charred corpse in the truck was not his. The police too were in on the game.

Noodles refuses the job. For him, who continues to call Max "Mister Bailey" and pretends not to recognize him, his friend Max died many years ago.

As Noodles goes out into the night, he thinks he sees Max,

but a garbage truck passes by and as soon as it is gone the avenue appears deserted. In the park, Noodles sees three antique cars full of people celebrating the end of Prohibition.

1933. Noodles enters the opium den above the Chinese shadow theater, stretches out on a mattress and begins to smoke with a smile of bliss.

[The scenes indicated by brackets, with a total running time of 31 minutes, were cut from the 1984 Italian commercial edition. They will be included in a restored version prepared under the direction of Claver Salizzato, with the assistance of Sergio Leone Production, Telepiù, and the Centro Sperimentale di Cinematografia Cineteca Nazionale.]

Upper photo: *Robert De Niro, alone with his remorse.*
Lower photo: *The rebuilding of the East End of 1923.*
Jennifer Connelly and Scott Tiler. **Opposite page***: Noodles (Scott Tiler) and Max as adolescents (Rusty Jacobs).*

A Fistful of Dollars was presented at the Sorrento Film Festival in 1964, but no critic noted its presence. *Once Upon a Time in America* is the big event of the Cannes Festival '84. It is very rare that a crime is honored by the cultural world. Maybe there were some who thought this was laughable. But if Olmi sought time past in a rural Arcadia, and Fellini looked for it in a provincial and operatic one, there is no obvious reason why Leone should not seek it in the black Olympus of gangsterdom – that is to say, in our past as spectators.

It was these films which gave us our rudimentary instruction in the willfullness of power (*Scarface*), in Machiavellian dealings *(The Rise and Fall of Legs Diamond)*, in disenchantment *(High Sierra)*.

Leone, the last virtuoso of the film tale, tenaciously conceived a summarizing of these myths. The preparation for *Once Upon a Time in America* occupies thirteen years of his life. Among the accidents along the road, were: the bankruptcy of a producer, the stealing of ideas by the competition, the monkey wrenches tossed in by the American unions during the shooting in the States, the cutting of whole sequences to meet the length agreed upon with the producer, the butchering of the American version which was cut by seventy-five minutes and re-edited in chronological order against Leone's will. Yet one cannot speak of an accursed movie, considering that the director approved the edition distributed in Italy and that the scenes originally sacrificed will be restored in the long edition. Another colorful aspect is the saga of the screenwriters who adapted Harry Grey's novel *The Hoods* – Americans and Italians, veterans and beginners, serious writers, detective story writers and movie buffs. In their pasts is a long row of milestones (as well as scandals) from *The Naked and the Dead* to *Rocco and His Brothers* and *Last Tango in Paris*. The credits also give Leone's name under the title "screenplay." For example, the idea of mixing up the new-born babies is not his, but it was he who, dissatisfied with the improbable idea in the novel for resolving the strike (the gangsters took dozens of their adversary-bullyboys out of circulation by giving them drugged whisky), put the problem in terms of a film memory: a solution was needed that was just as strong as the beheaded horse in *The Godfather*, but less ferocious, if possible. So the director functions as head playwright (like Ford, Visconti, Shakespeare...). The length too was established by the director: 3 hours 38 minutes, a provocation in the era of the remote control button.

The Hoods is an autobiographical novel, the story of a small-time gangster told in the first person as in a diary, with its notes of hold-ups, homicides, blackmail, pastimes and ideas... and without forgetting to go back to first causes every now and then with slices of Jewish life and debates between the gangster and his journalist brother. The film is more novelish than the novel itself. The life of Noodles, which in the book only included adolescence and youth, is prolonged into old age and told in flashback, multiplying memories and comparisons among the three stages of life. In the book the three boys surprise the local cop having sex underneath the stairs with Peggy, the Lolita of the building complex. They ridicule him and threaten him and let the incident go at that. In the movie the tryst takes place on a roof terrace where Peggy goes to hang out the washing. The boys photograph the couple in a compromising position, then blackmail him into giving them back the watch and obtain his complicity in their future crimes and access to Peggy's charms for free. Thus the episode is a reference point to a before and an after, and introduces the themes of blackmail and desire... in short, is placed in a context.

Certainly a roof terrace is not as miserable as a place below the stairs, but the roof terrace with washing hanging out is a traditional place of promiscuity in public housing: nothing is better suited to telling a story of survival and celebrating the ferocious vitality of little delinquents. The movie is full of such by now archetypal images: the Chaplinesque gag about the charlotte russe; the romantic, Fitzgerald-like dinner of the nouveau riche; the actress taking off her make-up in front of the mirror (Mizogouchi, Preminger...); the car that goes flying into the river as in *Jules et Jim;* the Bergman-like "wild strawberry" patch (that here is a toilet); and even the pilgrimage to the crypt à la Joseph Roth. (But the various hold-ups, shoot-outs, beatings and prisoner exchanges are all clichés, worn out and a little too Western-ish.)

Almost no historical factors disturb this compilation of myths (the part regarding the connection between labor unions and gangsters is the least inspired in the movie), nor do ambitions to present such iron-clad heroes as Cagney, Bogart or Mitchum. Noodles is a run-of-the-mill type who is not aware of it, a dreamer who goes through fundamental life experiences such as sex, love, friendship and adventure with an honorable vocation to defeat.

Noodles (Robert De Niro), like a traveler through time, chooses the period in which he wants to live and, once again young, finds refuge in a 1933 opium den.

In *Some Like it Hot,* Billy Wilder evoked the Roaring Twenties through transvestism and the confusion of the sexes. Leone goes further and confounds the impulses. Erotic desire is identified with anal instinct (Peggy and Noodles petting in the toilet); with gluttony (Patsy who gives up Peggy for a charlotte russe); with death (love-making in the hearse which recalls the flirtation among the sarcophagi in *The Colossus of Rhodes*). In the orgy, identity is both lost and found again: Carol only recognizes the four bandits once they have covered their faces and unbuttoned their pants. Here perhaps the absolute is being pursued along the road of dissipation.

But Noodles, who is secretly reading *Martin Eden,* is also

attracted by the American dream of happiness-beauty-energy which he finds in the form of the aspiring ballerina Deborah and her charms. She graciously grants him the first kiss between two Biblical verses. But when, bleeding, he knocks at her door, she remains stock-still and haughty as if she were acting out the end of *The Heiress*. Ten years later Noodles invites her to dinner in a seaside restaurant that has been opened only for them (in the novel it was crowded), but when she rejects him irrevocably he shows less class than Gatsby and rapes her. (Who is one supposed to feel sympathy for? The glacial victim or the infantile brute?) As an old man, Noodles finds himself in a theater admiring Deborah in a play by Shakespeare, just as when, as a child, he spied on her dancing from his hiding place in the bathroom. He has realized that the only place in the American dream for him is as a spectator. The criminal adventure is expressed as an experience of limitations, where violence borders on voluptuousness, terror on the burlesque, omnipotent power on impotence. The big thug runs after the little thugs as in a slapstick comedy, but this time the upshot is a dead man; the hold-up ends with Noodles raping a masochistic secretary; the gangsters blackmail the police chief by mixing up the baby boys with the baby girls (a confusion of orifices, an anatomical carnival); destiny is symbolized by a garbage truck.

Another myth, the one of male friendship, is celebrated here with a play of shoddy complicities, cruel jokes and false betrayals which outline the characters of the loser and the winner – sometimes a bit forced, as in Max's madness. But it is only at the end, probably inspired by Chandler's *The Long Goodbye*, that the theme of friendship becomes wrapped in a veil of myth. After thirty-five years Noodles discovers that the Machiavellian Max has taken him for a ride; and as punishment refuses to recognize him and to kill him as requested. Only then does Noodles cease to be run-of-the-mill and behave like one of the stoic heroes of *noir* films.

How is it that this eccentric saga manages to involve us, to become our past? Everything depends on how time is measured. Scarface made the pages of the calendar fly with machine gun bullets in a pathological version of American activism (in those days gangster stories were also success stories). Noodles prefers madeleines.

And Leone gathers together all the delights of the cinema of memory: symmetries, circularity, retrospective clarifications and violent juxtapositions. The structure of the movie allows us

Dirty-faced angels. Noodles and Max beaten up by a rival gang (above). The same one in the clandestine distillery (below). Scott Tiler and Rusty Jacobs.

A touch of neorealism. **Left:** *Noodles and Peggy, the Lolita of the building. Scott Tiler and Julie Cohen.* **Opposite page:** *A terrace with laundry drying, cliché of the promiscuity in the buildings of the poor. Julie Cohen and Rusty Jacobs.*

to be two Noodles at once: the one who acts and the one who remembers, the joyful gangster and the melancholy Jew; and to go through his life cycle at a solemn and dizzying pace, but without the uneasiness and absurdity of those old movies where the characters grow old from one scene to the next. Thanks to the flashback, two minutes in the present are enough to cover a leap of ten years into the past.

Noodles' life seems to be made up of significant moments rhythmically connected to each other. From one epoch to another encounters are renewed (the two returns to Fat Moe's), the goodbyes (in front of the prison and at the station); repeated lines (Deborah's "Mother is calling"), objects (the watch), activities (Max polishing his shoes) and songs ("Amapola"). Each repetition, always in a different key, traces the course of the years and also includes us in the circuit of the characters' memories and feelings.

But the lurches with which Leone shortens the thread of time are more surrealistic than pathetic. We visit the station, and a folk mural on the wall in 1932 magically becomes a 1968 pop mural. And another no less fanciful detail: the ticket-taker with a white beard is replaced by a young rent-a-car employee. Another gauge of time, accelerated and inoffensive, are the wrinkles on the faces of the characters. One cannot fail to notice that they are young people made up to look old, contrary to what was done in *The Man Who Shot Liberty Valance*. In growing old, Leone's heroes fulfill their destinies as archetypes, becoming their own masks. At twenty-three, Peggy

is even creamier and more luscious than she was at thirteen; Max at sixty seems like an even greater scoundrel than he did at twenty-three. Fat Moe never loses his tame and subservient look. Deborah finds eternal youth in the theatrical guise of Cleopatra. These irreducible adolescents never seem to grow up. Maybe they reproduce by cloning. David, Max's son, is the exact copy of his father (the actor is, in fact, the same one) as if he had been generated without the union with a woman. This is an expedient to strengthen the surprise in the scene where Max reappears, thus sparing a few lines of dialogue, but insinuating the suspicion that the present is a time of ghosts and simulacrums.

Other clues: the garbage truck, inspired by a true circumstance in the Jimmy Hoffa case and turned into horror fantasy by the fact that the driver is invisible; a Frisbee thrown

The struggle for survival.
Above: *Scott Tiler and*
James Russo.

by an unknown hand... In a word, the present no more improbable than the past. To be more exact, the present does not really exist at all. If the 1923 and 1932 episodes are flashbacks from 1968, it is equally true that 1968 is a flash forward from 1932 and the old Noodles is a projection that the young Noodles had had in the opium den. There is only the past as seen from the future and the future as seen from the past, memory mixing with fantasy with no points of reference.

It is always the pulsation of feeling that expands time. Leone goes into slow motion during a flight of street urchins and prolongs the end of a sequence dwelling on the pensive hero (an adolescent on the terrace, an adult at the seaside); he uses music to make memories blossom and to temper feeling (the bellicose march softened by panpipes).

Before and after prison.
Above: *Scott Tiler.* **Right**: *Robert De Niro and James Woods.*

The acting too obeys an inner rhythm. Like the hieratic kiss of the two adolescents, the ineffective attempt of Noodles to hide his embarrassment as he stirs a spoon in his coffee, the pilgrimages to Fat Moe's and the cemetery where the hesitations of De Niro suggest senility, disorientation and emotional upheaval. Nothing could be better for an epic of memory than this falsely lethargic actor hiding a distant hilarity in the depths of his eyes, as if behind the gangster there was a dormant actor.

The construction of the space contributes to this magical atmosphere. Leone could not ignore the fact that even the most deprived of his spectators had entered a Chicago speakeasy and driven the streets of the city in a Ford Model T at least once in his life. The extra emotions he offers are connected to traveling

Above*: Ready for action (James Woods, Robert De Niro, James Hayden, William Forsythe).*
Opposite*: A broken dream. Elizabeth McGovern and Robert De Niro in a scene filmed on the Lido in Venice.*

Gangsters and unions. **Above***: Treat Williams, Robert De Niro, Richard Bright, William Forsythe.* **Opposite page***: Treat Williams and James Woods.*

through time, to immensity, and they tend to make us accept even the less vital parts of the story. The opening of every sequence is a curtain rising on perpetually different, dated and expanded stages: in height (the opium den with its bunk beds); in width (the house facing the prison); in depth (the restaurant on the seaside). Or else they are vaguely spectral like the deserted slaughter house and the outskirts with its beached tugboats.

Space is stretched in all directions, but for acceptable reasons. For example, to film Noodles taking Carol bent over the table, there was no more sober and appropriate angle than a

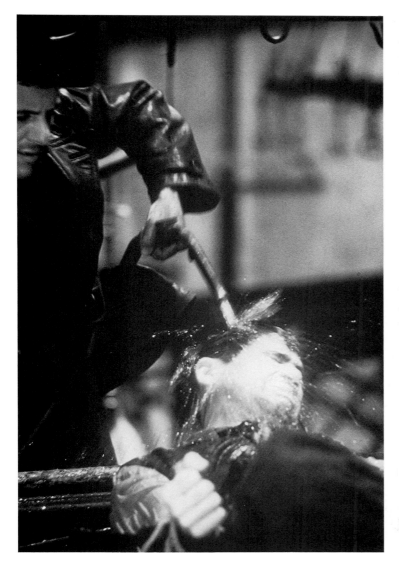 

frontal one, but with an upward view of the elegant coffered ceiling suggesting the "majesty of the vulgar."

The dolly shot that elicits applause (and, if you will, tears) is the one that begins the sequence of old Noodles' return to Fat Moe's. Through the window we see the old bar owner answering the telephone and sending away the last customers. Meanwhile the camera is elevated, broadens its angle to take in the semi-deserted street and drops onto a telephone booth to shoot a close-up of Noodles talking on the phone. Thus the movement of the camera suggests mystery and ritual by transforming this street corner into the theater of a furtive

ceremony in nostalgia which only we are able to understand.

Even the filmmaker's use of color evokes nostalgia, and this device is particularly effective in the seppia photos adopted for the 1923 scenes.

In certain moments of ecstasy and terror there is a tendency to the non-figurative, to white on white: the adolescent Deborah dancing in the back room of the bar among the flour sacks; Noodles who murders a killer in the factory in a flurry of feathers.

After the various deaths, rebirths, regressions and disillusions, the trip of initiation climaxes in a striking narrative

Opposite page*: Taking the law into their own hands (James Woods and Robert De Niro.)* This page*: The night of betrayals.* Opposite*: Tuesday Weld and James Woods.*

An impossible contract. James Woods
and Robert De Niro.
Opposite page: *A man all alone.*
Robert De Niro leaving the movie.

short circuit. In the same shot we see the Noodles of 1968 and three cars full of revelers in 1933 celebrating the end of Prohibition. Like a time traveler, Noodles chooses the epoch in which to live and goes back, rejuvenated, to take refuge in the opium den of 1933. The end generates the beginning. That is enough to suggest the infinite.

In the final shot, De Niro directs an ecstatic and crafty smile right at the public which is destined to endure as one of the memorable acts of anti-stardom along with Jean-Paul Belmondo's dying wink in *Breathless* and Marlon Brando sticking his chewing gum onto the railing in *Last Tango in Paris*. A disconsolate homage to artificial paradises: opium probably stands for the cinema (there is a Chinese shadow theater below the opium den) with its low-cost dreams and interchangeable

lives in which we are allowed at times to lose ourselves, gaining an illusion of immortality – even when the lives are as unfulfilled as Noodles's.

And since Leone liked to make comparisons to the classics and did not hesitate to slip the opening lines of Proust's *Remembrance...* into his dialogue ("What have you done with yourself in all these years?" "I have gone to bed early"), it would not be inappropriate to evoke the last line of *A Sentimental Education* to characterize the bitter irony of the epilogue to this movie. When Flaubert's hero takes stock of his life, he remembers an inconclusive adolescent visit to a brothel and considers: "We never had anything better, afterwards."

Sergio Leone died of a heart attack on the night of April 30, 1989.

SIX WAYS TO AVOID RESEMBLING JOHN FORD

Elizabeth McGovern in Once Upon a Time in America.

Actors

The Western owes a lot to the star system. It transformed the heterogeneous mythology of the Frontier into a concentrated pantheon of figures familiar to the public and capable of expressing themselves with ease and sobriety. (The intense mobility of Gary Cooper's face may even go unobserved.)

During the fifties even intellectual Actors Studio types played in Westerns – unusual roles like Paul Newman's neurotic Billy the Kid in Arthur Penn's *The Left-Handed Gun*.

Leone makes a blend of these styles, juxtaposing wooden exponents of understatement (Eastwood, Bronson, Van Cleef, Coburn) with disciples of Lee Strasberg (Steiger, Wallach) in the roles of Mexican bandits. Sometimes Visconti actors (Paolo Stoppa, Romolo Valli) appear in secondary roles, and occasionally Buñuel favorites (Fernando Rey, Margarita Lozano).

The best of them is Eli Wallach who enriches the ribald nature of his character with subtle shadings. When his brother the monk reproves him for not having helped their parents ("You didn't show up for nine years"), he replies by mimicking him three times ("nine years, nine years, nine years") varying the intonation from contrite, to distracted, to infantile in order to make light of his guilt. Here the histrionics of the actor mix with those of his character. Wallach evidently knows how to act with his whole body, even when shot from above, as he shows when he races around the cemetery looking for the grave. In one scene Leone makes him act in the nude, or rather nude with a pistol. Immersed in the bath tub, Tuco kills a rival by shooting him with a pistol hidden in the suds. Then he gets out and cautiously looks around the room, a beast of prey and of the theater. There is as much of the spirit of Boccaccio here as in the auteur nudes of Pasolini's *Decameron*.

Rod Steiger is more academically histrionic in *Duck! You Sucker*. His bravura moment is his long description of the Mesa Verde bank when he is twisted up in a fit of ecstasy ("not a bank, *the* bank, the biggest, most beautiful, fantastic, formidable, magnificent goddam bank in the whole world")

and groping with his hands for the right word ("It's like... like... a sign of whatsit... of destiny"). And there is also the scene of pain in the San Isidro grottoes brought to dramatic peak by Leone.

Normally in Westerns when we come across the smoking ruins of a farm attacked by Indians, we discover the corpses of the victims through the eyes of the hero. But here we first see the peon who collapses onto a bench weeping, murmurs a few words ("Six... I never counted them"), rips the chain with the crucifix from his neck and ends by picking up a machine gun and walking heavily towards the mouth of the grotto. The reason for his despair is not totally clear, and consequently his actions take on an air of sacred mystery. Only when he has come out of the grotto do we, together with the Irishman, discover the corpses of his family members while off screen the chatter of the machine gun is heard.

Romolo Valli in **Duck! You Sucker.**

Alongside such refinements Leone is capable of breaches of taste, primarily in the choice and direction of the secondary characters. In *Once Upon a Time in the West,* the threatening actions of Frank's henchmen, when they intimidate a little guy who wants to bid at the auction, are too theatrical to seem furtive and make the whole scene seem unreal.

There are some memorable provocations: for example, Lee Van Cleef striking a match on Klaus Kinski's hump. John Ford also liked emphatic gestures, but he filmed them with greater discretion. In *Stagecoach,* for example, one gets a glimpse of Thomas Mitchell in long shot who, having refused to toast with the banker, pours his whisky into the fireplace, causing the fire to flare.

Costumes

According to Roland Barthes, a theater costume has two duties: "to be a humanity," which means to give veracity to the character; and to be an "argument," which means to express the symbolic function of the character.

In Westerns perhaps the best humanity-costumes are those of Howard Hawks's drunkard sheriffs (Dean Martin in *Rio Bravo* and Robert Mitchum in *El Dorado*). A worn-out, much "lived-in" jacket and an undershirt which bear witness to the characters' decline and makes more dramatic the effort needed to rise again. In synthesizing the characters' past and present, costumes fit them like a second skin.

Among the most memorable argument-costumes there is the one of the captain-reverend Clayton played by Ward Bond in *The Searchers.* He goes nonchalantly from the horseman's overalls to the long, black formal coat and is almost never seen without the top hat that gives him the menacing and slightly ridiculous aspect of a totem. In the same film John Wayne

Mario Brega, Leone's fetish actor.

Clint Eastwood, the man in the poncho.

Lee Van Cleef

122

wears a civilian shirt and military trousers: he is a veteran and still considers himself a warrior. In brief, the epic dimension of the American Western can also be read in the accessories.

In the Italian Western, the costume is a often piece of folklore. In the dollar trilogy one remembers Clint Eastwood's poncho. In *The Good, the Bad and the Ugly,* the hero only wears it in the final duel like a bullfighter's costume. But in *Once Upon a Time in the West* the clothes are all dusty, threadbare, archeological, something never seen in American movie costumes.

The star system, as we know, always preferred the seemingly true to the real. Even with regard to hair-dos. With all-too Victorian ringlets, braids and chignons, the faces of the stars would seem less familiar to us. That is why, for example, Calamity Jane's hair-do in the two versions of *The Plainsman* (Jean Arthur and Abby Dalton) are inspired by the feminine fads of 1936 and 1966 rather than the fashions of the 1800s.

But Leone is historically accurate even when it comes to doing Claudia Cardinale's hair. At times, however, authentic detail creates an atmosphere of legend: for example, the famous overalls borrowed from *My Darling Clementine* which give the bandits a rapacious air.

Sometimes the costumes can have a narrative function (Harmonica ripping Jill's clothes to make her sexy and confuse the bandits lying in ambush) or an allegorical one (Jill, who, when in the desert, renounces the frills of city fashions).

Or they can become the objects of semiological comments on the part of the villain. Having to punish one of his lazy and incompetent henchmen who begs to be trusted, Frank makes the disparaging crack: "How can I trust someone who wears a belt and suspenders – someone who doesn't even trust his own pants?" Then he executes him with a kind of poetic justice: three shots, one in the belt and two in each suspender.

This is far from the provincial and prudent good sense of the Americans. In *The Big Carnival,* Kirk Douglas placated a newspaper editor with these words: "I have lied to men who wear belts, and I have lied to men who wear suspenders, but I would never be so dumb as to lie to a man who wore both a belt and suspenders."

Sets

No one seems to have noticed that in *Johnny Guitar* Joan Crawford keeps a bust of Beethoven in her office. The fact is

that the Americans did not emphasize. Even sets obeyed the rule of understatement. Starting with those wooden villages that had a saloon, a bank, a prison, a barbershop and a drug-store all lined up along Main Street, there was always something interchangeable about them, not to say pre-fabricated, despite the fact that they were inspired by period illustrations.

In Leone's villages, on the other hand, there is no growing civilization to honor, no drugstore, no courthouse and no (or almost no) inhabitants. They look like ghost towns and, sometimes, like Southern Italian small towns. The prevailing connotation is the archaic. The same is true of the interiors. The relay post in *Once Upon a Time in the West* is a kind of caravanserai that combines saloon, dormitory, blacksmith's shop and stables. At times one breathes the air of a museum or antique shop there. Leone, whose hobby was collecting antiques (mostly silver and Roman furniture of the 1600-1700s), finds ingenious narrative pretexts for showing off his rare pieces. He is even capable of turning a tobacco box or a clothes press into bizarre instruments of torture. The *pièce de resistance* of the antiquarian style is, of course, the private railroad car in *Once Upon a Time in the West* with its lace trimmings, brocades and brass handrails.

Leone's movies never lack a groaning board. In American pictures, if food was sometimes inscribed in a moral system as the counterpoise to alcohol (in Anthony Mann's *The Far Country,* the good guys go to the restaurant while the baddies visit the saloon), in the dollar trilogy the scenes of conviviality partake of the baroque, steeped in violence and death. In *A Fistful of Dollars* the Mexicans play at target practice against a suit of armor while they dine; in *For a Few Dollars More,* the bandits' bivouac in a deconsecrated church near a statue of an angel. In *The Good, the Bad and the Ugly,* Angel Eyes offers Tuco dinner before torturing him.

In *Once Upon a Time in the West* there would seem to be some need of precise period research. As Cheyenne listens to Jill, in order to make his role more active, rather than doing something like smoking, he eats stewed potatoes and peas from a little terracotta pot using a match for a fork.

Even the finest idea for a set in the films of Leone has to do with eating. The farm tables of the McBain's, set for a wedding banquet outdoors (with red and white-checkered table cloths, a symbol of frugal honesty, according to Erwin Panowsky) are turned into funeral altars for the bodies of his family members,

The private carriage in **Once Upon a Time in the West.**

historical frescos from becoming pompous. In Visconti's *Senso*, sets full of authentic pieces are filmed in a way to reveal their theatrical nature, since the heroine, without knowing it, is living through a melodramatic passion. Leone is exotic like De Mille and theatrical like Visconti. He even manages to make the desert theatrical. In *Duck! You Sucker* Juan and Sean have lunch seated on Louis Vuitton chairs set up in the middle of a Mexican sierra; *in The Good, the Bad and the Ugly* Tuco shades himself with a violet-colored umbrella as he escorts his prisoner across the desert. (An allusion to metaphysical painting: Leone loved De Chirico and had some of his works in his house.)

But the set that best represents Leone's taste is the stone arch with a man hanging from it in *Once Upon a Time in the West*. Here the nostalgia for the West becomes a romantic, obsessive love of ruins whose most illustrious precursor was Giovanni Battista Piranesi, the creator of the famous engravings that depict Rome's eroded centuries-old monuments from imaginary perspectives. Leone did something of the sort for the heroes of American legends, portraying them magnified by memory, corroded by irony and pursued by the shadow of death.

Dialogues

"Biondo, lo sai di chi sei figlio tu? Di una grandissima puttaaaaa—" ("Blondie, do you know who you're the son of? Of a great big bi-i-i—"). At this point the chorus of the Cantori Moderni di Alessandroni pick up and prolong the final vowel in a short musical phrase that imitates the howl of a coyote. In this way, both triumphantly and chastely, the phrase "son of a bitch" officially enters the list of uncensored epithets.

Way back in the time of *The Great War* (1959), Leone's three scriptwriters (Age, Scarpelli and Vincenzoni) already managed to get an insult like "faccia di merda" (shit face) past the censor by making it a patriotic act. (Gassman said it to an Austrian officer, thus showing that he preferred to die rather than be a traitor.)

This Rabelaisian taste is a constant factor in Leone. His Westerns have tragic images and comic dialogue. Certain lines seem written in order to be learned by heart. Everyone remembers Volonté's maxim in *A Fistful of Dollars:* "When a man with a pistol meets a man with a rifle, the one with the pistol is a dead man."

underscoring the profound unity of the farmer's life cycle: feasts, flour and funerals.

This erudite taste is shared by two predecessors, who are obviously very different from each other: De Mille and Visconti. De Mille loved to fill his scenes with period gadgets (for example, the sort of rudimentary cocktail shaker used by Jean Arthur in *The Plainsman*). In this way he created a kind of period color, a rather naive kind of exoticism, which kept his

Macabre humor abounds in *For a Few Dollars More*. After a short poker game where no bets are placed and Clint Eastwood beats an outlaw, the outlaw asks: "What were we betting?" And the imperturbable hero replies: "Our necks." Even the villain is humorous ("Rather than have that pair behind you, it's better to have them in front of you, horizontal and preferably cold").

The Good, the Bad and the Ugly has particularly funny and witty dialogue. In the prologue, the entrance of the hero is accompanied by a good line. One of the bounty hunters that has just captured Tuco observes the reward announcement and comments: "Your face looks like that of somebody worth $2,000." "Yeah," the blond guy says as he enters the scene with the camera at his back, "but you don't look like the one who's going to cash it in – a few steps back, please."

The whole movie abounds with naughty remarks ("Put down your pistol and put on your underpants"); or boastful ("I'm off, I'm going to kill him and I'll be back"); with threatening aphorisms ("The world is divided into two kinds of people: those with a rope around their necks and those who cut it... those with a loaded pistol and those who dig – you dig"); sadistic pleasantries ("I like guys like you because they make so much noise when they fall").

In *Once Upon a Time in the West* the humor is more subtle, putting courtly language into the mouths of naive persons (just as conventionally happens in operas).

Harmonica recounts a shoot-out, describing the bodies of the dead enemies as if they were a set of Russian dolls that fit one inside each the other: "I once saw three overalls like that some time ago. There were three men in them. In the men there were three bullets."

And sometimes he took pleasure in aristocratic reflections:
HARMONICA: And so you have discovered you're not a businessman after all.
FRANK: Only a man.
HARMONICA: An old breed. More Mortons will come and make them disappear.
FRANK: The future is something that no longer concerns you and me...

One could imagine one was listening to the Prince of Salina: "We were the leopards, the lions. Those who take our place will be jackals and sheep and all of them, leopards, lions, jackals and sheep will continue to consider themselves the salt of the earth."

Before dying, Cheyenne will leave a spiritual testament: "You know what, Jill? If I were you I would bring those boys something to drink. You have no idea the joy a woman like you gives a man, even just to look at her. And if one of them touches your rump, don't take any notice and let him do it."

Whereas in Ford's films men and women reach out in a chummy and mischievous way to spank each other's behinds, Leone's heroes philosophize about it as well.

Editing

There was a time when Hollywood directors took an attitude towards technical aids that some men take towards prostitutes: they enjoyed their favors in private while in public they pretended not to know them.

For them editing had to be invisible, fluid, functional to the story. Therefore movement from close-ups to long shots always had to be gradual and the actors never looked us or the camera straight in the eyes but always gazed to one side. In that way they eluded the boundaries of the screen and the presence of the camera, creating depth and continuity, and thus realistic effects. (Yet how many small, exciting discontinuities in the films of Hitchcock, Tourneur, and even Ford!)

But in Leone's movies, techniques are not entirely invisible. Forbidden link-shots from close-up to long shot, etc. are common. One of the most famous examples of this style is the three-man showdown used in *The Good, the Bad and the Ugly* narrated with the interminable repetition of three increasing enlargements (three faces, three cartridge belts, three pairs of eyes, three hands on pistols, then eyes and hands again, faster and faster). There is no real suspense since each new piece of information contains nothing to make us change our expectations about the outcome of the duel. It is pure 'filmic' tautology. Even if the trick is so utterly exposed that Leone – with the compliance of Morricone's music and its bursts of drums, trumpets, guitars, reminiscences of the "Deguello," anticipated explosions – finally involves us in the game of prolonging the wait beyond all reasonable limits.

But in *Once Upon a Time in the West* this dilatory technique works on behalf of the mythological element. The close-ups seem like true icons: Bronson's lined face in sculptured profile as suits the last remnant of an extinct race ready to be engraved on a coin; Henry Fonda's aristocratic face in which a latent uneasiness throbs. One would never tire of looking at it, all the more since the duellists are intent on preliminary maneuvering

Aggressive editing. Henry Fonda and Charles Bronson in **Once Upon a Time in the West.** *Below: The Good, the Bad and the Ugly.*

A nod to Soviet silent films is perhaps intended at the beginning of *Duck! You Sucker* where the arrogance of the rich who despise the peon is made grotesque by editing – in repulsive details of their mouths and fragmentary echoes of their insults that hammer away like futuristic captions ("ugly... like niggers, niggers... animals... idiots... brutes..."). One does not know whether the source is Eisenstein or Grosz, but one cannot but recall that in Ford's stagecoaches the descriptions of the relations among the social classes were more concisely described – John Carradine offering his silver cup to Louise Platt while refusing it to Claire Trevor who has to make do with drinking directly from the water bag.

But Leone's unusual style does not only regard editing. The zoom, if sometimes used in a banal television way to underscore feelings where a simple linking shot from the same angle would be better (Marisol embracing her child during the exchange of prisoners in *For a Few Dollars More,* and the bandit on the train who notices the presence of Cheyenne in *Once Upon a Time in the West*), makes us think in at least one case of the comics (even if the zoom does not exist in the comics). When Ed McBain sees his daughter fall, hit by gunfire, and before running to help her cries "Maureen," Leone zooms onto his shouting mouth rather than his eyes, suggesting a degree of dismay not to be expressed through traditional mimicry.

There are also plenty of subjective camera shots, with their unfailing effect of disorientation. In identifying ourselves with what a persons sees, we lose control of the scenic space and are swallowed up.

(the villain circling around the good guy so that the sun will be in the other's eyes) like a macabre dance. Here the slowness does not weigh on the spectator.

This predilection for editing in particulars also includes an involuntary homage to one of his first teachers of theory, Lev Kulesov. In *For a Few Dollars More,* the two bounty hunters study the announcement of the reward on El Indio. Blondie looks at the amount while Mortimer observes the picture of the bandit and the words "Dead or Alive," a sign that the former is motivated by money and the latter by hatred. The significance does not depend upon the acting but only upon the order in which the four shots appear. This is precisely a Kulesov effect.

In *A Fistful of Dollars* there is a subjective camera shot of the dying villain where the site of the duel becomes more and more blurred. In *Duck! You Sucker* too, there is a subjective camera shot that allows us to look death in the face – that is to say, the firing squad lined up in front of Juan. And in both movies there are also some voyeuristic subjective camera shots where someone unseen spies on a scene of violence. But the most dislocating subjective camera shot occurs in *Once Upon a Time in the West* and announces the entrance on scene of some new character (the McBain child who comes running out of the farm during the massacre, Cheyenne who appears at the auction). Leone assigns us their field of vision even before letting us know who the person is.

The movements of the crane also reveal small differences in comparison to the transparency of the Hollywood style. For example, the dolly shot of the title scene in *Singing in the Rain* follows the movements of Gene Kelly and at the same time, creating a certain dizzy feeling, involves us in his euphoria. In *Once Upon a Time in the West* the technique, rather than enhancing the feeling, actually create it. We know nothing about Jill when she gets off the train; but after the majestic dolly that follows her walking through the unknown town, we have felt the loneliness she will have to face and the courage which she probably has to face it with.

All of this does not exclude a very classic sense of continuity when called for. In *For a Few Dollars More*, after the semi-serious duel in which Mortimer and Monko have shot their hats full of bullet holes, we see the two hats and two cartridge belts placed on a table as a sign of truce. In fact, the camera pans the two leads seated at the table in friendly conversation. At the beginning of *The Good, the Bad and the Ugly*, Blondie has freed Tuco from the three bounty hunters and the latter is already exulting over his hair's-breadth escape. But now the hero, without saying a word, pushes a cigar into his mouth rather than untie him. In the following shot we see Blondie delivering the Mexican up to a sheriff to cash in the reward. The gesture of mockery was like a punctuation mark that permitted the transition between the two scenes. A gesture of that kind can sum up the meaning of an entire episode – Tuco ends the hold-up of the old arms dealer by sticking a sign saying "open" in his mouth – or even of an entire picture (the harmonica that Bronson pushes into the mouth of the dying Fonda in *Once Upon a Time in the West*. Sometimes the link between two sequences can be an object (the book by Bakunin that Sean throws away during a bivouac and which the pursuers

find). It can also be a rhythmic analogy: the slapping rhythm made by the Union officer as he cleans off his uniform is echoed by the marching rhythm of the prisoners in the concentration camp; or a referent of sounds: Sean in Dublin shooting at the English patrol links up with the gunfire of the Mexican platoon, Frank is about to shoot his pistol at the McBain child when there is a cut to the whistle of the train Jill is traveling on.

Even less classical and more maneristic than these shock ellipses is the use of alternating editing in the first two Westerns. In *A Fistful of Dollars* the pistol shots exchanged by the Rojos and the Baxters has in counterpoint Joe in the cellar knocking with the butt of his pistols (he was the one to trigger the gunfight) on the barrels, as he hunts for the treasure. At the end of *For a Few Dollars More* El Indio, in order not to share the loot, sends his men out to risk death on the streets of Aguacaliente and the editing alternates shots of the bandit wearing a bored expression waiting to find out the result of the battle and shots of the gunfight in which the two bounty hunters kill off the Indian's men. In both cases the irony subtly corrodes the suspense giving rise to something that could be called "alternating editing with a Machiavellian content." A veiled form of detachment. Leone, more simply, would say it was "the puppeteer's game as an extra excitement."

Music

Even before Leone, Westerns had something operatic about them. For example, the highly codified nature of the story elements, the amount of musical interludes provided by singing cowboys, and the musical commentary in the orchestral background. John Ford integrated musical folklore very well into the dramatic structure giving dancing scenes the function of aggregating provisionally different ethnic and social groups (*Wagonmaster, Fort Apache*) and used classically inspired compositions to go from the adventurous to the epic – as in the case of Max Steiner's emphatic, largely brass score for *The Searchers* which gives a martial tone to the odyssey of the two heroes.

In Leone the music (written by Ennio Morricone) carries even more decisive weight. In *A Fistful of Dollars,* for example, the irony is suggested mostly by the title theme which comments on Clint Eastwood's astute tricks.

Charles Bronson in Once Upon a Time in the West.

music-box motif), that suggest feelings the images alone cannot evoke (when Jill enters the station, the theme for a solo voice expresses the loneliness of the woman from the East coming into contact with the West but also alludes to the director's nostalgia for that lost world). And sometimes the music takes audacious liberties, as when the sentimental tune ("Sean... Sean... Sean") is used as commentary for a massacre and during the collapse of the bridge in *Duck! You Sucker.* There is a realistic pretext for this (Sean put cotton into his ears to protect them from the explosion), a psychological meaning (the dynamiter's memories of Ireland) and an unexpected sense of sweet catastrophe (Kubrick was just as audacious at the end of *Dr. Strangelove* in eroticizing the atomic mushroom with a languid song of Vera Lynn's). No less Dionysian is the music just before the end of *The Good, the Bad and the Ugly* when the "ecstasy of gold" theme transforms Tuco's rush to the cemetery in search of the treasure into an ironic icon of cupidity which encompasses the spirit of the picture – and perhaps of all Leone's pictures – funereal Bacchanals to exorcise the melancholy of the story.

Probably Morricone sees the Western from an even more barbaric and amused point of view than Leone does. One knows that he loves eccentric instrumentation: anvils, bells, whistles, whips, shots, animal noises, human voices used as instruments and passages from Bach and Mozart. It could easily become pleonastic, but everything is so well amalgamated into the sound texture of the film that it is hard to distinguish the natural noises from those electronically imitated, the realistic from the symbolic. For example: those percussion sounds that accent the Mexican's panic as he waits with a noose on his neck in the epilogue to *The Good, the Bad, and the Ugly...* are, in reality, nothing but amplified heart beats. It may happen that the orchestra hides among the actors (the music box in *For a Few Dollars More* and the harmonica in *Once Upon a Time in the West*) or that music replaces dialogue (Harmonica cracks on a note to provoke Cheyenne). Similarities to pure melodrama are contained in the use of emphasis and in the ritual quality of certain scenes, but they are also present in the leitmotifs that follow the characters with unusual precision (the Cheyenne theme stops abruptly at the very instant of his death), that transform their character according to the situation (in the horror-style flashback of the rape scene in *For a Few Dollars More* the music seems like a tormented version of the

The Name Above the Title

At times the language of credits has its own esoteric effectiveness. *Per un pugno di dollari:* regia di Bob Robertson; *Once Upon a Time in America:* a film by Sergio Leone. An inverse symmetry that encompasses twenty years of Italian cinema from mimicry to nomadism.

The difference between "directed by" *(regia di)* and "a film by" has lost the heraldic value that it had in Hollywood. (Frank Capra called his autobiography *The Name Above the Title.*) But Leone, who controlled every phase of the production of his movies, would have been entitled to the name above the title even in those days. All the more so in that the results bear the imprint of a highly personal taste.

Let us list some of the constant factors:

1) A space that deliberately eschews unity, always too cluttered or too empty, with *very close* close-ups, wrinkled and immobile (evoking masks), and long shots where the depth cracks open suddenly.

2) A subtly entranced rhythm (enervating dilations, traumatic ellipses) sustained by a fusion of drama and music that makes one think of opera.

3) A story evoked in flashbacks, in which a ceremonial tone (highlighted in duels, long waits, and farewell scenes) takes priority over plot construction.

4) A mannerist tendency to exalt popular genres and themes with tragic, precious, solemn and recondite treatment.

5) The insistence on reviving past epochs (the West, Prohibition, but also in unrealized projects like those on Leningrad and the seventeenth century) with a scrupulously realistic and arbitrarily chimerical style.

6) A continuous flowering of Mediterranean mythologies: Trastevere swaggering, rustic vendettas, lacerating martyrdoms, obscene pranks... (Giulio Bollati has written that Christ and Pulcinella are the key figures of the symbolic Italian stage).

A more rigorous critical period would have cited Auerbach to compare Leone to the late Roman, Ammiano Marcellino and Apuleius, of whom he speaks in a chapter in *Mimesis* ("personages who constantly live inebriated on blood and in fear of death... mixtures of the most subtle rhetorical arts and a strident and contorted realism... a prevailing of the magical-sensual over the rational-ethical...").

Today one tends to agree with Baudrillard who called Leone the first post-modernist director. No one, perhaps, expresses skepticism about the representation of reality better than this Roman who, in his early films, thought he was celebrating the American legend of the 1800s and instead ended up describing primarily the Italy of the sixties already resigned to its cynicism. He did it with less subtle shading than greater directors, but also with fewer inhibitions.

In the snapshot album of the boom era, together with Mastroianni pretending to enjoy himself at a party, and Alain Delon who only feels he is alive when he is playing the stock market, and Vittorio Gassman who feels young when he is at the wheel of a sports car, there should definitely be included the scene in which in a desert clearing a man with a gun meets another man with a gun. They are joined by a third man and the three, in order to avoid sharing the loot, prepare for mortal combat, studying each other at length, spasmodically at length – in order to make us understand that they are astute and ferocious, to give us time to listen to the music, and because they think that in the West that was how things were done.

THE LEONE METHOD:
OTHERS ON LEONE

The villain, to humiliate his partner, kicks the man's crutches from under him. Probably inspired by Edward Dmytryk's Warlock. *Henry Fonda and Gabriele Ferzetti.*

Dario Argento

The Sense of Rhythm

I followed the usual course of so many kids who love the movies, without thinking that movies were something one could actually make. Then I began to work as a critic, and that was how I met Leone.

As a critic I had reviewed his first films for *Paese Sera* (a leftist Rome daily, *Ed.*). We did a lot of talking and he was struck by my love for cinema. Politics was all the fashion among the kids of my generation and not many of us loved American or French films or knew what a traveling shot was. Leone loved talking movies to me, and I was crazy about talking to him, learning how certain shots had been achieved. And so the desire to be a director took hold of me.

Usually at the start of professional life there is a moment when you cross paths with a certain personality. This does not mean that you necessarily are influenced to the point of becoming a carbon copy, but you will be able to learn some secrets, the alchemical secrets of cinema, of rhythm, of narration, of the great machinery. I think this has also happened to a lot of my colleagues: it is the fatal encounter that serves to break the ice – the maestro breaks it and you get to see what there is below. If you get your start with mediocre people everything becomes that much harder because you learn the vices, the stupidities of minor films. For my part, I had the good fortune to be at Leone's side. I don't think he intended to be my teacher. He is not someone who surrounds himself with pupils, but his expertise imparted itself.

Leone had a natural instinct for pinpointing talent (even his films which seem to be so highly constructed are actually very instinctive). He goes by impressions, by looks; he understands what goes on inside people. For writing the screenplay of *Once Upon a Time in the West* he had the courage to choose two talents that were still budding, like Bertolucci and me – he, who could have had the world's greatest screenwriters, took two semi-newcomers. He understood that films were changing.

There was a need of people who did not tell the usual story in the usual way. In the script we included the images, the sensations. Being virgins for all practical purposes, we had a lot to say stored up, things that had stratified inside us over the years.

The fly inside the pistol was my idea from a film that I was supposed to have made with Duccio Tessari. But when there are three of you writing a film together it is difficult to remember who came up with what ideas. That experience taught me what to do when I start a movie and want to express something inside of me. One talks a lot, one talks vaguely about a story idea, then one brings everything into the discussion – what are movies all about, what is happening right now, what were the last films you saw like. You dive in and stay there, maybe for weeks at a time. You talk about this dolly shot, you remember that old movie, all just to get the motor going.

I learned a lot listening to Leone talk about cinema. Narrate concrete events, as Hitchcock says, for whom even the nightmares had to be realistic. I was still too naive. He brought me down to earth. Leone is no theoretician. He used to say: "No, the public doesn't like that kind of thing." He taught me to keep the audience in mind. We are storytellers, not prophets.

From him I learned that films are time, rhythm – and that thought obsessed me to the point that in my work I time everything with a chronometer, even when it is not necessary. And I learned to use the camera for narration, with continuous interference from the author who behaves like a writer, individualistic even in his punctuation. I understood the character, the meaning of a boom, a dolly shot, of shooting from behind someone's shoulders, the author as one more character, present in every scene and making that presence felt as Godard does.

I never saw Sergio on the set. At the time of *The Good, the Bad and the Ugly* I walked into the mixing studio where he was inserting the cries of falcons into the shot of a valley. He tried many, but none of them satisfied him.

Immediately after writing the script of *Once Upon a Time in the West*, gripped by a strange fury, I began my first film, but I don't think it is important to see a director working on the set.

A director's ideas do not appear like subtitles and there is no time to give lessons in directing. To learn, I think one must sit by his side while he is preparing the movie at his desk.

When I made my debut with *The Bird With the Crystal Plumage,* I followed Sergio's example and hired many beginners, among them Vittorio Storaro whose first color film it was. Everyone told me: "You are a beginner, you must work with solid professionals." I thought the opposite. Just because I was a beginner, I didn't want people who would interfere, profiting from my inexperience. But I called on Morricone for the music. To use a lot of music, in every way, make it part of the story, record it before shooting – these are other things I learned from Sergio. But for *Profondo rosso* [Deep red] I took the Goblin, four kids who hadn't yet done anything. They had studied the Yes in England and had made a very beautiful recording. The oldest of them was twenty. Such adventures bring their rewards; Sergio was right.

I love him very much, even if we never see each other. There is no need to be together all the time to love someone.

Nino Baragli

They Called Him "the Pulveriser"

I call Sergio "the Pulveriser" because he reduces you to a pulp when the editing starts. But working with him is more exciting than with the others. When I edit a film of his I don't think about it only when I am in front of the Moviola, but also when I am watching television at night. There is never a sequence that you can shoot in a couple of hours. You need at least a day, and then the next day when you take another look at it, three other solutions present themselves. With him "duplicates" do not exist. You may take one line from one take and one from another which you thought was going to be discarded. Sergio shoots a lot of footage because he has a taste for the shot, because he wants to get the maximum out of the actors, because he wants to cover himself. There are a thousand ways to edit a film of his; certain scenes can become dramatic or ironic according to the editing.

Here we have 300,000 meters of footage of which at least 200,000 are to be edited. Sometimes Sergio bangs the clappers

as many as eighteen times. Then when he stops De Niro starts: "Now let's do one for me." When we have to cut because the movie is too long, we never cut within a scene, we cut out whole blocks, because the rhythm must remain the same. You mustn't confuse rhythm with speed – in that case the editors of TV commercials would be the great masters. Instead, you need much greater ability to edit slow tempos because it is harder to find the right spot to cut. It's easier to cut a battle scene. Sometimes we try to cut fast, but in general the results are rather modest. In *Once Upon a Time in America* there are some fast sequences, for example a shoot-out with the gunfire concentrated on an automobile where there are shots eight or ten frames long. But they alternate with slower sequences.

It is hard to keep up a fast rhythm for an entire film. Certainly there are movies with fast editing like *Star Wars* which can be successful, but they are soon forgotten. *Judgment at Nuremberg* lasted three hours and yet I would have been happy if it had been three hours longer. Leone is a very visual director. The right-hand side of his scripts, is much less full than the left, with sets, situations, states of mind. I'm not crazy about movies that talk too much. My habit is to edit with the sound track and then see the scene again silently and I have to understand everything without the dialogue. That way I am sure I did a good editing job. One of Leone's best scenes, the one with the opening titles of *Once Upon a Time in the West,* was entirely without dialogue, only effects created during the editing.

It does not matter if sometimes there are some wrong cuts: what counts is the feeling and that there should be something in the eyes of the characters. At one time you could not cut from a long shot to a close-up. With Sergio we do it all the time. When Pasolini made *Accattone* the editor refused to do the job because, according to him, the film could not be edited. Pasolini did not understand the technique of linking-shots. He made a long shot of someone running and then, when he had to change to a close-up, instead of making the linking-shot while he was moving, he let you see him when he was already still. He was a writer who used the camera like pieces of paper where you can make corrections and cancellations... And still I managed to edit the film which was successful even if there were some wrong cuts.

In general I prefer to do the editing by myself. Directors bring the set with them to the Moviola – they all do. If an actor made them suffer they would gladly cut out everything he did, even if he is excellent. "He was drunk – you weren't there that morning." "I wasn't there and the audience wasn't there. When they see him on the screen they'll like him." I edited *La notte brava* [Brave night] in four days and four nights, sleeping half an hour each night, because the producers, who were young and had no money, had to deliver the edited movie by a certain date in order to get financing from the distributors and finish the shooting. Bolognini saw the edited film and did not change anything. From that day I edited all his movies. I edited *Everybody Goes Home!* while Comencini was still shooting it.

Sometimes while editing you can find solutions that no one thought of during the writing or the shooting. For Comencini's *La tratta delle bianche* [White slave trade] I got the idea of putting the pelota scene before the credits.

And yet editors are never mentioned by the critics. No one knows their names except people in the profession. Do you say it is hard to know where the responsibility of the director ends and the editor's begins? Well then, all you have to do is come and see us work.

Elizabeth McGovern in **Once Upon a Time in America.**

Bernardo Bertolucci

Under the Sign of Visconti

For me Leone has always been the genius among the directors of popular films. I have found in them a mixture of great vulgarity along with great sophistication, an unprecedented case in the history of Italian cinema. I, coming from the Nouvelle Vague, felt closer to Leone than to other Italian directors. The first time we met was in a movie theater. I had gone to see one of his films at the first showing on the day it opened and he was in the projection room to supervise. He saw me and after a few days called and we made an appointment. I was going through a very difficult period. Years had passed since I had made *Before the Revolution* and I had not managed to shoot another movie. The prospect of working with a director like Leone excited me very much. I said something that perhaps may have won his heart. I told him I loved the way he shot the horses' asses. Only a very few American directors have an eye for that. And he immediately began to tell me the beginning of a story. Dario Argento was there too. We worked

together and developed a long treatment almost without any dialogue. Then I received a proposal to do an episode from *Amore e rabbia* with the Living Theater. I wanted to shoot something of my own, so I quit that team.

I remember that in *Once Upon a Time in the West* there was a part that was miraculously similar to what I had written. It was when the family is awaiting the arrival of Claudia Cardinale and are preparing the cakes on tables out of doors. I remember several pages I wrote describing in great detail the chirping of the cicadas interrupted by disquieting silences and then the white dust of the bandits who suddenly appear from out of the cornfields. I had written cornfields because I associated the West with my Emilian countryside.

Apropos of geography, looking at a map of the United States for a name to give to the town, I found one I liked very much: Sweetwater. Last year when Michael Cimino showed me the long version of *Heaven's Gate*, influenced a little by Leone and a little by *1900*, he told me: "We shot it at Sweetwater." It is really a strange coincidence.

Leone knows American movies very well, and I played around, filling the treatment with allusions (to other films). In

"One part miraculously resembled what I had written; it was when the family was waiting for Jill McBain (Claudia Cardinale), putting cakes on the tables outside." With Frank Wolff in **Once Upon a Time in the West.**

those years making allusions had become a cult, and I said to myself: how nice it would be if a director of Leone's talent made unconscious allusions rather than deliberate ones. Maybe I managed that in a few cases.

The hardest part was making Leone accept the presence of a female character. I remember suggesting a scene to him. "The hero enters a kind of whorehouse, throws himself down on the bed and tells the girl: 'Take off my boots.' And she does. 'Massage my feet.' And she begins massaging them." And this should be the beginning of an erotic relationship. Leone interrupted me. "Yes, she massages his feet, slowly, slowly... and he falls asleep." His tendency was to neutralize the possibility of sexual relations.

He has an extraordinary ability for visualizing his fantasies. For example, the treatment said that Claudia Cardinale appears for the first time getting off the train dressed in the latest New Orleans fashion. Leone says: "The carriage door opens, detail shot from the carriage steps, her feet come into view, then her skirt covers the camera and we note that she isn't wearing underpants." It seemed a very fine idea to me: a character who was immediately identified by her sex.

Leone was always full of ideas, inexhaustible in making transformations, a great perfectionist. I got on very well with him because our relationship with our ideal models was somehow similar. In me, it came from much reading of Bazin and the French; in him it was perhaps more direct; but in any case my way of seeing American Westerns when I was a kid in Parma, going to the movies on my bike, must not have been much different from Leone's way of seeing them in the Trastevere movie houses; the fever in our eyes must have been at the same temperature.

I too used the legendary Hollywood names, Sterling Hayden, Lancaster... I put them rather more in quotation marks. For me moviemaking has always meant making movies that ask just what movies are. So, unfortunately, for me the allusions are more conscious. Both of us were influenced by Visconti, even if my Visconti was more the interior one rather than the Visconti of the fluttering curtains. Mine is the melodramatic Visconti, the one of behavior carried to excess and also of a certain guilty class consciousness. I think that, for Sergio, Visconti is more a point of reference for elegant sets, for example, the carriage at the beginning of *Duck! You Sucker*.

Now I am trying to do a film taken from Hammett's *Red Harvest* which has a plot a bit like that of *A Fistful of Dollars*. I remember proposing it to Leone in 1969, but he was more

interested in making *Once Upon a Time in America*. It makes me happy that he is shooting a gangster movie and a movie in two parts like *1900*. It means that our elective affinity continues. I believe that Sergio's movie will be more psychological, while *Red Harvest* will be in the style of an Elizabethan tragedy with music by Kurt Weill – a great gangster carnival.

Peter Bogdanovich

Two *Beeg* Green Eyes

An American actor I know, once had a passionate romance with a Russian ballerin a though neither of them spoke the other's language, and it lasted just as long as they didn't know what they were saying to each other; as soon as they did, the affair terminated abruptly. Strangely enough, the language barrier between director Sergio Leone and me didn't have quite the same result, though probably if we'd understood each other from the start, I would have seen less of Rome than I did.

This all happened in late 1969. Leone, the father of the Spaghetti Western (the Clint Eastwood ones beginning with *A Fistful of Dollars*) and the *padrone* of the extreme close-up, had, through United Artists, asked me to direct the first movie he was to produce only, rather than direct and produce. With assurances from U.A. that they would welcome radical changes of the first draft of the Mexican Revolution script I had received, and firm promises that Leone would really function only as producer and therefore leave me to make the film as I saw fit, and taking into consideration that it was a free trip to Italy, where I'd never been, and bearing in mind that I hadn't made a picture for well over a year, that three projects I'd been preparing had fallen through, remembering too that a baby had just made us three and that the specter of having to go back to writing articles was hanging over me, I accepted, you might say, reluctantly.

In those days, Sergio didn't wear a beard; in fact, he was a rather unimpressive looking guy – medium height, pot belly (usually with a cashmere sweater pulled down tight over it), hardly any chin to speak of. But he met me at the airport with the majesty of a Roman emperor expending a bit of largess on a worthy, if nonetheless decidedly inferior, underling. It was subtle, the feeling behind that first meeting, but the impression

Scene from **Duck! You Sucker.**

was confirmed in the weeks that followed. Actually, Sergio wanted me to believe he was a great director; *he* didn't believe it, which is perhaps why it was so important that those who worked for him did. I had only just liked a couple of his movies, so it was a difficult act for me to play, though for a while. I tried to imply admiring thoughts in the *way* I said things rather than in *what* I said, most of which I guess was negative.

Luciano Vincenzioni, the writer of Leone's two best films (*For a Few Dollars More; The Good, the Bad, and the Ugly*), had been hired to work on this one too, and he and I got on famously right from the start, though his job was the not very appetizing one of being translator, mediator, arbiter, and scenarist all at once. Luciano, by the way, is everyone's ideal Italian – he could be exported as a tourist attraction – charming, gracious, enthusiastic, good-looking, and funny. For some reason best known to himself, he really wanted me to direct this picture – a lot more than I did – and much of our time alone together was spent in his trying to get me to be more politic with Sergio. Our script conferences were usually called for 11 A.M., at which time I would arrive at Luciano's apartment and we would wait for Sergio. Around one o'clock he would call to say he'd be a little late so why didn't we go out and have some lunch. About three o'clock we'd return and Sergio would arrive promptly at 4:30 for two hours of work. After a couple of weeks of this, Sergio inexplicably presented *me* with a watch (an old one of his) – presumably to keep him from being late – a joke I made and Luciano *says* he translated.

Anyway, the conferences would usually begin with my complaining about the title of the film, which was *Duck! You Sucker* (The Men at U. A. had assured me it had to be changed, though I don't believe they ever bothered to tell Sergio this; but then they probably didn't refer to him as Benito to his face

either.) Sergio would carefully explain that "Duck! You Sucker" was a common American expression, to which I would reply that personally I'd never come across it before. I would then point out that the substitution of an "f" or the transposition of the "s" could result – in English, anyway – in some rather less than polite expletives. In answer, he would say that this title was in his view an Americanization of a well-known Italian expression, "*Giù la testa, coglioni,*" which literally translated means, "Duck your head, balls," and which he intended to use as the Italian title, with the "*coglioni*" part left off. I said the idea sounded splendid, but that while this Italian saying probably received immediate recognition from his countrymen, "Duck! You Sucker" would not have the same effect on Americans. Well then, he would say – this conversation really *did* happen more than once – what *was* a comparable American expression? I replied that I couldn't think of one quite as colorful, but that we were known to say things like, "Watch it!" or "Hit the dirt!" or "Heads up!" or "Look out!" or even, simply, "Duck!" This was met with incomprehension and distrust from Sergio, who I'm sure was becoming convinced I wasn't a real American at all.

Most of our time, however, was taken up with plotting. Sergio would begin each new sequence with a rush of English and much acting, all of which he did in the middle of the room accompanied by dramatic gestures. "Two *beeg* green eyes!" he would invariably begin, one hand leveled above his eyes, the other below to indicate what we would be seeing on the screen – a shot I could easily picture, as I'd seen at least a score of them in every Leone movie. "Cut!" he would continue. "Foots walk!" And all attention would now focus on his feet as they moved purposefully forward. "Clink, clink," he would say, providing the sound effects for the spurs. "Cut!" he'd *yell* this time. "Hand on gun!" he'd whisper, grabbing his hip. "Cut!" Hands would zip back to frame his face. "Two beeg green eyes!" and so on, until a burst of gunfire sent him reeling into an armchair, spent and panting, both from the physical exertion so soon after eating (in Italy, and particularly with Sergio, almost any time of day is soon after eating), and the pure inspiration of the sequence itself. He and Luciano would look at me for a reaction, which early in these conferences I would attempt to make one of enthusiasm but which inevitably moved into something closer to exasperation. After all, it had always been my assumption that a director planned out his own sequence of shots, and I had the distinct impression that Sergio expected me to shoot everything just as he was acting it out. The climax of this particular part of our negotiations occurred late one heavy afternoon ar Sergio's home (sometimes to avoid waiting six hours for Sergio, Luciano and I agreed to drive the hour it took to get to his house in the suburbs and work there instead). Sergio had just begun a fresh scene – "Two beeg green eyes!" – when I interrupted to say that I wished we could just discuss the action instead of the shots and, besides, I didn't like close-ups anyway. When this had been translated, there was an amazed and deflated look on Sergio's face. A long pause followed. If I didn't like close-ups, he finally asked just a bit ominously, what *did* I like? To which I perversely replied, "'Long shots." Driving back to the city, Luciano shook his head in wonder. "You are crazy," he said. "This man make his whole career on the close-up and you say you don't like the close-up. I think you don't want to do this picture."

But my favorite story-conferences began with Sergio making a dramatic and terribly serious entrance – six hours late – and warning us not to forget that the movie we were making was really about Jesus Christ. I believe this was occasioned by a new set of reviews Sergio had read from France or the American avant-garde which searched out the hidden religious symbolism and significant nuances in his latest film, *Once Upon a Time in the Far West*. For over an hour, at least once a week, therefore, Luciano and I had to listen to a lecture on how the Irishman in this movie, *Duck! You Sucker*, was really a metaphor for Christ. Luciano had to listen, that is, since the lecture was in Italian, and after the first time or two, he spared me the translation. I would usually place my hand on my brow, meditatively, in order to shield my eyes in case they inadvertently closed for too long a time.

Luciano would eventually bring Sergio down to earth and things would liven up. The best times were spent watching Sergio act out his most cherished moment in the picture, which had to do with the Mexican bandit passing wind while holding a lighted match to his posterior. Sergio particularly relished making the sound both of the initial departure of wind as well as of the subsequent one caused by the meeting of visibile match and invisible gas. After acting it out in splendid detail, Sergio would collapse in sad exhaustion in his chair, shaking his head about the pity of not being able to do this on the screen, at the same time threatening to do it anyway. If there had been a great deal of this sort of thing one day, it was invariably followed the next by a sobering account of the film's actual religious import.

I had left Los Angeles in October, planning to stay abroad until at least April to make the film. I was home for Christmas... It was a Sergio Leone movie without a doubt, and that's who should be directing it, I told U.A., which is ultimately what happened, though Sergio first found a young Italian director to take my place. To be honest, I think Sergio was about to fire me when I left, having no doubt decided by then that I was going to shoot the entire film in long shot. As it turned out, however, after two weeks of Leone's pushing buttons on his Italian surrogate, the stars, Rod Steiger and James Coburn, refused to accept the situation, and so he finally had to direct it personally.

This year, a similar thing happened when Sergio hired an inexperienced Italian fellow to direct another Western, *My Name Is Nobody,* with Henry Fonda. After a while, circumstances again forced Leone to take over, though, finally, I'm afraid that's what Sergio wants; if the picture then turns out to be a bomb, he has the excuse that it was not really his plan to make this one and that he'd been forced to come in and do the best he could, at the same time postponing the major work he was preparing. In other words, exactly that crisis of self-confidence I had suspected four long years ago. When all those critics and people say you're good and you don't really believe it, at some point perhaps the thought of being found out becomes overwhelming and you would rather retire underfeated than face failure. Actually, if this perhaps presumptuous deduction is true, it is a considerable pity, because Leone is often a very good director. My experiences with him prove nothing except that directors should never collaborate. It is, as Mr. Mailer has well described it, a totalitarian job. And *Duck! You Sucker?* Well, after an initial release failed to spark much interest, a quick title switch was made to *A Fistful of Dynamite,* but that didn't help. The French critics loved it, though, as did several American ones. I quite liked it myself – all but the serious parts. I had enjoyed those more when Sergio acted them out himself.

Claudia Cardinale

A Sweet and Penetrating Look

I have wonderful memories of *Once Upon a Time in the West.* On the first day of shooting at Cinecittà we began, contrary to custom, with a very delicate scene, the love scene in bed. Our positions were very uncomfortable because we had to hold our

Sergio Leone, Claudia Cardinale, Tonino Delli Colli on the set of **Once Upon a Time in America.**

faces as the camera work called for (Sergio used several cameras); and the bed was suspended.

Making things more complicated was that I did not know Henry and he had never shot such an audacious love scene before; and on the set that day were all the journalists in the world – it was like being on a theater stage. I had to ask for the reporters all to leave and then we were alone with just Sergio and the cameraman, Tonino Delli Colli, who is a truly lovely person. Two strangers meet on a set and suddenly find themselves together in bed. It is quite embarrassing, especially because there was Henry's wife sitting right in front of us and

watching closely. Later we became very good friends.

Henry was a very solitary type. He was always standing around by himself and his relations with people were very precarious, but he was an extraordinary person. You only had to know him to love him. He was always detached, loved silence, painted pictures. He had a beautiful way of moving; I don't think anyone could ride a horse like him; he seemed to be a part of the horse.

Charles Bronson is also a very solitary person. He sat around with his cap pulled down over his eyes just so as not to see anyone and not to have to greet anyone. He always had a rubber ball in his hand which he bounced continuously. It is hard to get a smile from him. He got along well with me, maybe because I am introverted too.

It is very easy working with Sergio. We communicated by looks without having to say anything. His look is both sweet and penetrating. He betrays the tension he feels when he directs by always playing with something in his hands, a pack of cigarettes, matches... Sometimes I came up behind him and blocked his hands!

Sergio has a great love of actors and knows how to help them. He has a wonderful way of telling the story of the movie and has the music written before starting to shoot. Before beginning each scene he played the Jill theme and this helped me to concentrate, to remove myself from reality. It was like a magical way of becoming the character. Sergio shoots a lot of close-ups and it is much easier to act with the camera very close. After many films it has become like a friend to me: the way it hums is familiar to me, and I can feel at once if it is set up well or not.

Sergio is very demanding on the set, and it is right that he should be. Visconti was another you could never satisfy. At the end of the day's work I have to feel totally exhausted because that means I gave everything necessary – otherwise I am not satisfied. On the set everything must be very serene and relaxed; so for me it is important to have good relations with the whole troupe. When it is a serious set the technicians will rarely talk of anything else. There is a religious atmosphere when you shoot, a moment of great silence, great concentration, and everyone is involved with the movie. We actors are very sensitive, very receptive. To act you have to be in a state of grace and feel yourself surrounded with great love, great affection. I could never act with a director whom I did not esteem, who did not speak sweetly to me. Sergio is very sweet, very understanding with the actors, but he is very demanding with people on the set: the production, the assistants... He rehearses the camera movements for a long time, because the camera and the actors must become one; the movements must be very smooth, then the acting comes by itself. I don't remember ever repeating the scenes many times.

What I liked about my character, Jill, was her grit, her strength. She knows what she wants and sticks to it and wins. You don't find many women's roles like that in Westerns. With few exceptions the women have very limited roles in American Westerns. But in *Once Upon a Time in the West* Jill was the central character, everything revolved around her. I like the scene very much when Jill comes home and feels that there is something to discover, turns everything upside down, then stretches out on the bed and is photographed through a net like De Niro at the end of *Once Upon a Time in America.*

We shot in stupendous locations: Almeria, Monument Valley... lots of dust and heat, but it was necessary to get into the part. The movie has become a classic. They are constantly showing it in Paris. I went to see it again two years ago on the boulevards and the theater was full. I often hear the Jill theme being played even in the department stores.

When I met Jason Robards in the jungle on the set of *Fitzcarraldo* (he did half the film then had a nervous breakdown and we reshot everything with Klaus Kinski) we spoke nostalgically about our characters in *Once Upon a Time in the West*: his entrance into that kind of tavern is really stupendous. I remember having talked about it with Bob De Niro too when I saw him again on the set of *Once Upon a Time in America.* It was in Canada where I was shooting a film with Lino Ventura and we spent a lot of time together. I discovered that all the actors loved *Once Upon a Time in the West* and remembered every detail of it.

I often see Sergio; it's a relationship that goes beyond the set. I did several films with Luchino. With Sergio I could have done others because it is easier for a director to work with people he knows well. In *Once Upon a Time in America* I was supposed to play the part of Carol, the nymphomaniac, but then the movie was done in a New York style so the idea was dropped.

Tonino Delli Colli

Once Upon a Time Black and White

I met Sergio when I was working with Bonnard on movies like *Il voto* [The vow] and *Tradita* [Betrayed]. He was an excellent assistant director: he prepared the sets, chose the supporting actors... he was like a son for Bonnard. We met again many years later to make *The Good, the Bad and the Ugly*. Sergio and I understood each other very well; there was no need for a lot of instructions. We shared a point of departure, an aesthetic principle: in a Western you cannot use a lot of color. We kept to subdued shades: black, brown, off-white, since the buildings were wooden and the colors of the landscape rather vivid. In

Above: *Elizabeth McGovern and Tonino Delli Colli on the set of* Once Upon a Time in America.

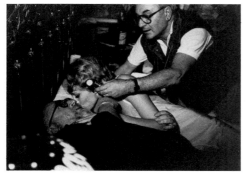

Left above: *Claudia Cardinale in* Once Upon a Time in the West.
Left below: *Sergio Leone, Darlanne Fleugel, Tonino Delli Colli* .

Once Upon a Time in the West we gave a sandy color to the whole copy. We like colors like these; we have the same tastes.

In *Once Upon a Time in America* we differentiated between three periods. For 1923, a sepia print that recalls the photos of that period. For 1930 we tried to keep the image as neutral as possible, a kind of metallic black-and-white, cold approach to the gangster films of that epoch. For 1968 no special effect. We used a little Rn, a special bath patented by Technicolor Italiana, which made the blacks more velvety, added brilliance to everything and reinforced the contrasts. At first Sergio thought of shooting in Cinemascope but after the first tests he changed his mind. Unfortunately the theaters are not adequately equipped for Scope. The lenses of the projectors make everything fuzzy and you need to create more contrast, use more incisive lighting, sharper photography, to get higher relief. In America we saw *Once Upon a Time in the West* on television: decompressed, reprinted, a real mess. So in the end we preferred to turn the television set onto black and white. No I really am not nostalgic for Cinemascope.

If anything I miss black and white a little, maybe because it was harder to use. The half-tones and the relief have to be created with light. I am one of the pioneers of color films in Italy. I shot the first movie in Ferraniacolor: *Totò a colori* [Color Totò]. It looked a little like a postcard. The public wanted to see full colors, as they were not yet used to it; and we had no experience. Ferraniacolor called for strong lighting because the film was not very sensitive. But I began to experiment with effects and found that the results were good even with a little less lighting. There was a development in the course of the shooting, one can see it easily, because the movie was shot in narrative order. The final scenes use a lighting that is not so flat, more precise.

Since then there has been a lot of progress in the use of color. Even the Americans have discovered natural lighting and often shoot with a light coming from above and the eyes in shadow. These are things that are all right for a single scene, but in the long run become annoying. We too use natural lighting but we also illuminate the face. We keep to a more classical style.

I believe the director of photography should be the main ally of the director, should realize his desires, give form to his ideas, coordinate the effects, the costumes... He should be asked to examine the locations because the director doesn't notice the light conditions, doesn't consider the fact that during the day the sun moves. With Sergio we did little preparation: he chose two or three alternatives for every scene, and then we had a quick look around to decide.

With Pasolini we would agree on a painter to coordinate my work with that of the set and costume designers. Leone sometimes would refer to a movie, but it would be hard to get to see it, and then it might not be much use because situations are different from picture to picture. Pasolini didn't know technique very well; the results you get from the various lenses. He would shoot everything panoramically, then a knee-shot, then a bust shot... he was a bit Chaplinesque. But Leone moves a lot; he shoots in movement. He has very precise feelings. A little movement that someone else might find insignificant says something to him. And when the film is shown you notice this. The audience is not aware of it on a technical level, but feels it psychologically. He shoots his films well, that's why the audience accepts certain slow moments. American actors, like De Niro, are also enthusiastic about his pictures. He works a little slowly, but the results are excellent. Furthermore this movie cost about half what it would have cost the Americans to make. To do what we do with eighty people, they need to use one hundred and fifty.

Sergio Donati

The Western as Religion

I started out at eighteen as a writer of detective stories. Tinto Brass based his movie *Col cuore in gola* [With your heart in your throat] on one of these: *Il sepolcro di carta* [Tomb of paper]. My first job in the movies was collaborating on the screenplay of Ricardo Freda's *Faite-moi confiance* [Trust me] from a novel by James Hadley Chase. Around that time I was approached by a young assistant director who looked hungry and went around in an old Fiat 600: Sergio Leone. He asked me to write a horror film taking place in a hotel in snow country. He had known a hotel proprietor who was curious about the spicy behind-the-scenes life of the movie world. I wrote the subject but it came to nothing. Anyway snow brings bad luck for the movies.

My books had been translated into a dozen languages but they didn't make me a living. So when I finished my law studies I went to Milan to work as a producer in advertising and I stayed there six years. I am almost prouder of the work I did in advertising than of the films I have written.

Leone phoned me every once in a while from Rome with improbable proposals. In '62 we went to Lebanon together for a few days to inspect a location. I wrote a screenplay, *Rebus,* that Nino Zanchin made into a film years later with the actor Anthony Harvey. One day Leone phoned me telling me to go see *Yojimbo* because he wanted to make a Western from it. I didn't believe in it and I didn't even bother going to see the movie. That's how I lost the chance to write *A Fistful of Dollars.* Then he asked me to write *Grand Slam*, a movie about a diamond theft he was supposed to direct. He had a contract with the producers Papi and Colombo for ten films at a ridiculous fee. On the eve of his departure for Egypt, Leone and the producers quarrelled and the movie was directed by Giuliano Montaldo.

I did a little ghostwriting *For a Few Dollars More*. For example, I worked on the scene of the little old guy who lives alongside the railroad tracks and I came up with Eastwood's last line when he adds up the amount of reward on the heads of the bandits lying dead in the street and notices that there is one missing: a line that got applause. In those days people applauded in the movies like they do in stadiums. In the end Grimaldi convinced me to give up my advertising work and come to Rome.

Scene from Duck!
You Sucker.

For *The Good, the Bad and the Ugly* Leone wanted the best screenwriters on the market so he recruited top comedy writers Age and Scarpelli and it was a mistake. They wrote not a Western but a kind of comedy with a Western setting; I think hardly a line they wrote got into the final version. The same misunderstanding recurred when Age and Scarpelli worked with Hitchcock on *Triple A*. He wanted a mystery and they wrote a comedy.

I worked for six months on *The Good, the Bad and the Ugly* and it seems to me that I performed several miracles. The picture was too long. Sergio never made the very common mistake of shortening a sequence by altering the rhythm. He preferred to cut out whole blocks of the story. After having cut out half an hour of story we completely changed the dialogue between Lee Van Cleef and the legless soldier, having them talk about the part that had been cut. And finally we worked hard to find the actor expressions that were suitable to this new dialogue.

We were all rooting hard for this picture. Since it absolutely had to come out before Christmas, Baragli and a few others of us had been sleeping on cots for weeks next to the Moviola. I risked being divorced by my wife. I noticed a curious metamorphosis in Sergio. Whereas he had always worked happily in previous movies, now he had begun to get neurotic, to fear that he wouldn't be able to live up to his reputation. Since he is not presumptuous and knows his limitations, he is always being assailed by doubts, tries to postpone finishing the film and even becomes personally unpleasant. We did the mixing of the last reel at 5:30 in the morning; so the first copy was ready the next day. We were all exhausted and happy after four months of killing work. The production inspector arrived with a bottle of *spumante* to celebrate. Leone got up, dodged past him and left with a laconic "good night." This is Leone the man.

For his next film he wanted to get off in high gear, so he completely forgot his promise to let me write the script and began working with Bertolucci and Dario Argento. After many months he phoned me: the two intellectuals had disappointed him. I was very offended and took the job just for the money. I wrote the whole script in twenty days, the second half without even getting up from my chair. I wrote the kind of script he likes with interminable descriptions, allusive dialogues, long biographies of the characters, and lots of suggestions for the direction. He always says, "Please don't forget about the cuts." We always have to suggest three or four different cuts so that he has a choice during the editing.

I fought against things that were kept in the film and which actually work well there, like the interminable scene in the saloon in the desert where nothing happens. With regard to the duel, I managed to get him to keep it shorter than in earlier pictures. I would even have kept it off screen and just showed Claudia Cardinale's reactions.

Then I went to Los Angeles with Sergio for the American edition of *The Good, the Bad and the Ugly*. The Americans are obsessed with invisible dubbing, so to create lip synchronization we changed all the dialogue. If someone says "pipa" they are capable of translating "pepper." So I stayed two weeks to supervise the English dubbing.

Sergio hated Clint Eastwood, I think because he had asked for so much for the last movie; each of them thought he was the reason for the other's success. Eastwood arrived at the dubbing studio with his old shooting script in hand and, to provoke us, placed it on the book-rest demanding to read that one rather than the new dialogue. A young vice-president of United Artists had to intervene, Chris Mankiewicz, Joe's son, threatening to keep him from ever making another picture in America. The Americans are capable of exchanging the most tremendous threats without blinking an eye.

Then Leone phoned me from Spain where he was shooting *Once Upon a Time in the West:* forty minutes had to be cut. When I got to the set I saw him in a crisis for the first time. He was shooting the scene on the McBain farm and he confessed to me: "I was sure I could shoot it with a different rhythm; I tried and couldn't manage it." So I stayed there and cut the script during the shooting.

While he was making the movie, I wrote the script for *Duck! You Sucker.* The role of the Mexican was written for Eli Wallach, but the movie was costly and the producers wanted a famous actor like Steiger, an actor I detest and who had nothing in common with the character. For the Irishman, I would have liked to have gotten Jason Robards. But though Robards was a great theater actor, one whom the cameramen applauded when he finished a scene, when you went and looked at the day's shooting the magic had vanished. He is one of those actors who, as the saying goes, doesn't get past the screen. He hasn't got the eyes. I think that's where the whole problem lies. I did the first draft of the script which was discussed in a meeting with a whole lot of people and Leone sided with them. To get even, I put in all the changes proposed in that meeting. Leone got annoyed, and we broke off for a year. Meanwhile Vincenzoni arrived who had been working by himself. Then came Bogdanovich and they didn't hit it off. Leone insisted on explaining how to shoot to him: "Here you do a zoom shot..." And he replies: "I never use zooms. I hate zooms." So Bogdanovich was fired.

A year later he called me and I rewrote the second version of the script; then we had another fight. It is tiring to work in this way. *Duck! You Sucker* is a movie I detest, maybe because it does not resemble my first version of it. It is a movie full of rhetoric, noncommittal; it even contains a quotation from Mao...

I also wrote two political Westerns for Sollima: *The Big Gundown* and *Face to Face*. The first was a good subject by Solinas set in Sardinia, the story of a *carabiniere* who pursues a bandit and in the end, after finding out that he was innocent, gets him in his sights and shoots. The story was moved to the West and given a happy ending, partly on Leone's suggestion.

Face to Face was too verbose. I hate films that preach, and then I don't think that ideology and Westerns go together. Sollima did too much sloganeering. He is more cultivated than Leone, someone who has done a lot of reading. Leone's culture is exclusively visual: he is a great movie lover; he could reconstruct from memory the scripts of *Vera Cruz* and *The Magnificent Seven*.

Leone is a great instinctive director, a great actors' director. He knows how to get everything out of the actors; he does not try to squeeze the actor into the picture or vice versa. There is an exchange between what the actor can give to the film and what the film can give to the actor. He is one of the few Italian directors who is really worth anything. Vincenzoni and I wrote a film taken from *Orlando furioso*. If Leone had directed, it would have become a cult movie like *The Raiders of the Lost Ark*. For him the Western was a kind of religion; he invented a rhythm, a world in which he believed. To believe deeply in something always bears its fruit in the movies.

At a certain point Leone became part of movie history and probably he did not feel the desire to make anything more. For a long time he flirted with the project of *Once Upon a Time in America*, but he realized that it meant measuring himself with a completely different narrative style. Gangsters cannot move like cowboys; they cannot take a quarter of an hour getting out of a car.

In 1967 I began doing preliminary research for this picture. I went to the archives of the *New York Times* to breathe the air of the thirties and I discovered, for example, that the front pages ran headlines like "Last Night Jack Legs Diamond Dined at 21." It was a little like telling the story of the Ciano family in Italy.

I confided my perplexities to Leone: what did we know about the Jewish East Side? It was as if an American director decided to recount the history of Trastevere in the thirties. There are the precedents of *The Secret of Santa Vittoria* or the Sicilian episode in *The Godfather* where everything has an incredibly false ring to it. The risks are enormous. At least Leone could get an American art director.

I read a version of the script. There was one great piece of ingenuousness: a gangster who disappears from Chicago in '33 retires to the provinces to cover his tracks and then resurfaces in New York twenty years later. This was possible in the West in 1833, but in 1933 with the FBI? No.

And then, who knows? A film can be splendid and not make a penny or vice versa. But nowadays we are in the hands of a bunch of adolescents who talk loudly at the movies. *The Return of the Jedi* took in $60 million in its first week. And that's nothing. The sad part is that popcorn alone earned $9 million!

Franco Ferrini

The Whole Memory of the Cinema

In 1971 I was commissioned to write a monograph on Leone for the publications of the Centro Sperimentale di Cinematografia. They knew that I was one of the few madmen, along with Bernardo Bertolucci and Glauber Rocha, who liked Leone's movies. At the time this taste was a little scandalous.

Leone was supervising the editing of *Duck! You Sucker* at that moment. He put me up in a Rome apartment (in those

days I lived in a small town, at La Spezia) and gave me a Moviola to see the shots. It was an opportunity to spend some time with him. I had the secret ambition of becoming a screenwriter; unlike many of my contemporaries, I didn't dream of being a director.

One evening, probably I was half-drunk, when Leone was taking me home in his brown Rolls Royce, I found the nerve to ask him to let me collaborate on the script for *Once Upon a Time in America,* and he accepted. That night I didn't close an eye... partly because there was an electric blanket which I could not manage to unplug and I was worried about its turning into something like an electric chair.

Leone wanted to use a book of novelized memoirs, *The Hoods,* written in Sing Sing by a Jewish gangster. But the author had sold the option to Dan Curtis, a producer-director of horror films. He did not want to give them up and this delayed things for years. So we started thinking of alternatives. One of them was *Mile High* by Richard Condon, the author of *The Manchurian Candidate,* which John Frankenheimer had filmed. For all practical purposes it was the story of John F. Kennedy's father, a financier who, during Prohibition, seems to have had relations with the underworld. But this writer needed years to write a screenplay and Leone was in a hurry.

I did research, I read many books on Prohibition: novels, gangsters' biographies, studies of the Jews. (One valuable book was *The World of Shalom Alaikem* by Maurice Samuel who reconstructed the life of a Russian village during the time of the pogroms.) European immigrants – Russians, Poles – thrown suddenly into the secularized American life tried to keep their rituals, their mythology; they reacted a bit like the Italians. There was nothing at all like the Black Hand, but there were many Jewish names among American gangsters. One example is Monk Eastman who was remembered by Borges in *A Universal History of Infamy.* Leone wanted to do a movie on Jewish gangsters at all costs. Weighing heavily on him was the shadow of the two "godfathers" that had dealt with the world of the Italo-American Mafia from every point of view.

In the end Grimaldi, who was supposed to produce a picture, got the rights to *The Hoods.* Norman Mailer was the first one called on for a screenplay. His script had a hallucinatory and fragmentary construction in flashbacks with continuous leaps in time that were almost incomprehensible and kept the story from taking on structure. In the final version all this coming and going becomes more convincing thanks to

the part played by memory. It is a rather Proustian structure. In Mailer it seemed a little like Resnais and not very suitable for Leone's rather solemn style of narration. Medioli and Arcalli did a very coherent treatment that became the skeleton of a script in which Benvenuti and De Bernardi also had a hand.

At first I had a complex about making mistakes. It was consoling to discover that these old hands at screenwriting had no such qualms. One could quote that old, banal phrase that the police say to people involved in murder cases: "Tell me anything that comes into your head, even if you think it has nothing to do with solving the case." That's the way a screenplay is written.

From the very beginning the film took on its own physiognomy, even in contrast to the book. The book was written by someone who knows the facts but who lacks a sense of the fabulous. We were all very much aware that we were not writing the history of gangsterism, but its mythology seen through European eyes.

Benvenuti and De Bernardi, besides writing *Amici per la pelle,* which displays a certain affinity with the childhood scenes of our film, have written various opera films; and *Once Upon a Time in America* also has an operatic construction. At the end, for example, there is a great dramatic scene that distinguishes it from all other gangster movies. When Noodles (Robert De Niro) returns to New York after thirty years of exile, he receives a mysterious invitation to a theater where they are giving *Anthony and Cleopatra.* In the dressing room he encounters Deborah (Elizabeth McGovern) who has become a great actress. As she is taking off her make-up he notices that the ravages of time have not altered her beauty, she really is like Cleopatra. The mask is the face. It was a very complicated scene to shoot because the actress has to take off her theatrical make-up while keeping on her movie make-up. Then the woman becomes the source of a dazzling revelation, on a par with the incest revelation in *Oedipus Rex.*

The film begins in dream terrain, in an opium den disguised as a shadow theater. It begins with the raw material of cinema: shadows on a wall. At the end, in 1968, De Niro leaves the party where all the survivors have met again, turns a corner, and with magical editing finds himself back on the last night of Prohibition in the Chinese quarter with a crowd that is going crazy. I remember a phrase of Scott Fitzgerald's where he says that the end of Prohibition was the end of the costliest orgy in history. In the end, Noodles goes and takes refuge in the opium

Robert De Niro and Elizabeth McGovern in **Once Upon a Time in America.**

den of the film's beginning. After having started out from a dream, after having gone through reality, New York in 1968, he goes to take refuge in a dream again. This strange itinerary of the movie is also a judgement on reality.

Leone always asked us to link one scene to the next, especially the connection from the present to the past and vice versa. He asked us to do the editing in the script; the links could be associative, traumatic, musical, or false links. He didn't want arbitrary flashbacks but ones motivated by the action. And in fact they are an innovation: a meeting point for the European memory narrative and the American action and behavior traditions. Maybe the loveliest of the links comes at the end when you pass from the Chinese quarter to a journey of no return, a final journey. In the script there is even a quotation from the final lines of Proust's *Remembrance of Things Past*.

Twelve years ago Leone had thought of a very original prologue to film in a sequence shot. A seaport wharf at night. Two men dragging a corpse with obvious difficulty. A

movement of the camera reveals the feet of the corpse embedded in a block of cement. It is a typical execution in the style of the American underworld. The camera follows the shroud as it sinks under water; at the bottom of the sea we find other corpses that have undergone the same treatment: men bound to automobiles, bejeweled women... Then the camera enters the course of a sewer, passes through a tunnel and we find ourselves in another underwater graveyard, a poorer one, with corpses bound to a railroad tie, to a cart... and this also reflects the division of New York into boroughs. At last the camera comes to the surface and the Statue of Liberty appears very white in the night; and we see the title: *Once Upon a Time in America*.

Unfortunately this sequence could not be realized because a few years later a film by Frankenheimer was released, *The Forty-Four Per Cent Death*, with Richard Harris and Bradford Dillman, that contained a similar scene. Thus the idea was born for a railroad grade crossing with a train full of cars of that

151

epoch, and then the idea of the Chinese shadow theater which Leone ended by cutting, reluctantly, partly because we had found something very similar in Peter Weir's *The Year of Living Dangerously.*

And here is the prologue that I thought up, a bit as a joke: a dark, slightly rounded object fills the screen. At its center something lighter in color can be glimpsed. The image comes more into focus: it is a man's head with a newly-shaved tonsure. His pants are slit in a strange way that show his bare legs. He is eating a succulent meal with great gusto. Two guards watch him through a spy hole. It is the last meal of a condemned man. Under the eyes of other condemned prisoners, he walks stoically down a long corridor without resisting. He is in the electric chair where they attach the electrodes to his head and legs and then proceed to the execution before a small group of spectators. The doctor makes sure that he is dead and announces the length of the death agony – a little more than a minute. It was not painless. As the protocol demands, two prisoners are among the spectators who are quick to spread the news by water pipe tam-tam. A revolt breaks out and the prisoners destroy their cells as we have seen in so many American movies. All the cells are opened electrically and their inmates ordered out. One of them is missing from the roll call. A guard stands in the entrance to his cell and sees an old man who is writing with a pencil stub on a toilet roll. "Goldberg, come on out!" (the name of the author of the book upon which the movie is based). But absorbed like a rabbi in his indecipherable writing, he does not obey. The guard pulls him out by force and now the toilet paper falls to the floor and rolls out like a papyrus scroll. On it we read *Once Upon a Time in America.* In my crazy imagination, all this was to be one very long sequence shot. Leone looked at me with indulgence and said it would have cost half a million dollars.

After many years I think I have finally understood what it was in his films that conquered me: his anti-neorealistic style. Leone is the only director who has never once set up his camera in front of the world in which he lives. He only shot pictures set in ancient Rome or the Far West. The year 1968 of this picture is the closest he ever came to portraying recent time; and it is no accident that 1968 is the most mythical year in recent history. It is this aristocratic rejection of reality that I find seductive.

Enrico Medioli

In the Beginning There Was a Novel

The first time I saw *A Fistful of Dollars* I enjoyed myself tremendously and left the theater full of admiration. No two films of Leone's are exactly alike; there has been a trajectory, a rising to greater maturity.

I think if Leone selected me it must have been partly because he wanted someone to contradict him. I had never made an action film. The idea of doing something far from my usual routine seduced me. It was like putting myself to a test.

In the beginning there was a novel, *The Hoods,* which cost a lot of money and little of which remained in the movie. We worked with Norman Mailer and he produced two long treatments which didn't work in film terms. It is one thing to be a writer and something else to be a screenwriter; they are two different professions. There were no new solutions, nothing that one might really have expected from Mailer, who is, himself, a New York Jew of humble origins, from the East Side I think.

Afterwards I worked with Kim Arcalli, Bertolucci's writer and editor, who died not long ago. He was a wonderful man. He did not write, he spoke for hours, came up with precious ideas; the crux of the film is his. Franco Ferrini also participated in this work from the start. Then Benvenuti and De Bernardi did another treatment. It is not the first time a lot of treatments have been done for a picture – I remember the case of *Rocco and His Brothers.*

When a long period of time is involved there are things that are written one year and are old by the next year. Cinema is written on water. For example, we had included an episode about a strike with allusions to the case of Jimmy Hoffa, the head of the truckers' union who had been involved in a scandal because he apparently made a loan to some Mafiosi, money coming from the union's pension fund which he put into some bad financial investments. At a certain point Sylvester Stallone's *F.I.S.T.* was released. It looked as if someone had read our script and copied it. But no, certain things are in the air and are ripe for use so that you have to keep up to date. And then maybe it was better that we avoided the historical and sociological aspects. We felt we might be interfering in a world that was not our own. It is already going far when a group of Italian writers make a movie about another country; to make political or sociological judgements would have been a little presumptuous. Certainly in *The Damned* we made judgements, but then that was a hell observed with wide open eyes: it was the classical Visconti theme of a family's personal hell.

And so we reached the definitive script, which was very long and had to be cut. We went to New York to inspect locations. Then there was the translation to be done. Leone wanted an American writer. The two screenwriters who first worked on it tended to make too many changes in our script; so we turned to Stuart Kaminsky, an execptional writer of mystery stories, a New York Jew.

It is the story of a group of boys from the East Side of New York who make up a little neighborhood gang and who as adults become gangsters, but without ever becoming part of a big organized crime ring; they remain independent. Everything is seen through the eyes of one of them, the only survivor, who goes in search of a certain time lost in the past.

Time is another important element of the film and it is played out on three levels: when the heroes are boys of about thirteen, when they are young men, and finally when the survivor, Noodles (Robert De Niro), returns in his private quest. The story has several women characters and a love story in which the time motif again unfolds. It is an American world revisited with European eyes, a black fable told in very realistic terms, but the archetypes are these: the gangsters, the gangsters' girls, Prohibition, cruelty, the great male friendships, and tragedy.

These were all things that we knew from films. None of us was American, none of us a Jew, none of us a gangster; but we had gotten all of it, filtered through cinema rather than through literature. The secret thread that winds through the movie is a more European one. The sense of certain mistakes made, of deceit, of treachery, of bitterness, of time that is irremediably lost. There is also a side which is fun, overbearing, rash and headstrong which belongs to twenty-year-old boys who are criminals but also heroes.

The book narrates chronologically, whereas we start off in a youthful period and from there branch out into childhood and old age. The things I like best are these transitions from one epoch to another and from one age to another for the characters. I think they contain a certain emotional force. They are resolved very realistically. For example, the old Noodles goes into a bar where, as a boy, he used to hang out; and through a window he sees Deborah dancing as a little girl. He sees her directly, without crossing fade outs; and a moment later we see

Noodles, too, as a child again.

The book ends with 1933, and contains nothing about old age, while the movie ends in 1968 – for no particular reason, possibly just to let it be understood that afterwards things would be slightly changed.

Leone stuck quite close to the script; there was a lot of hair splitting over the lines. Visconti gave you more latitude. There were infinite numbers of meetings, then everyone wrote; sometimes even Visconti wrote. Visconti had fine ideas for cuts. It was his idea to end *The Leopard* with the ball scene rather than with the death of the prince, as in the book. Leone did not write, but he followed our work closely: he rejected, accepted, modified. As a screenwriter he was the exact opposite of what he was as a director. In the script he wanted everything to flow, he didn't want pauses, perhaps because he knew that in shooting he would drag out the tempos. Then too, in this movie, besides his slow tempos there are those of Robert De Niro. It is no accident if the original film lasts four hours.

The point of departure for our work was a great love for old American movies. I adored them when I was a kid, but now I do not feel like seeing them again; one might be disappointed. It is part of my culture. My high school professor was Attilio Bertolucci, Bernardo's father. He was an exquisite professor of Italian, but he also spoke to us about Joan Crawford, about John Ford. He could never see *Stagecoach* without becoming excited about it.

Of course, unlike ours, movies like *Scarface* were made at the time of the events they depicted. Today there is no one who is capable of handling Mafia or Camorra stories with the same punch. Maybe some B-movies have a certain power and realism despite their moralizing. I think that seen again in a few years' time they may render the idea of a particular Italian world.

As models for my work I have the great novels of the 1800s. I like a story that grabs you. Today, unfortunately, everything that is incomprehensible and boring is often considered intelligent.

Ennio Morricone

Towards an Interior Music

When Sergio came to my house to commission the music for *A Fistful of Dollars*, I recognized him at once: we had been classmates in third grade and I remembered that we had both been rather lively children.

Little by little we found a way of understanding each other. Sergio did not express himself in a musically very precise way. Anyway, there are always problems of communication between a director and a composer. Also, on the piano you cannot always make clear what a piece is going to sound like when it has been orchestrated. Sometimes we spent whole days getting through to each other: we were both saying the same thing, but in different ways. There were never any serious misunderstandings, however. We had long, lively talks to get our opinions across to each other, and then we reached a compromise. The danger is when there is no discussion and you do not even try to understand the other's point of view.

In composing the music for Leone's movies I deliberately ignored the American precedents. In general the Americans use symphonic music even for Westerns, something I never do. I find symphonic language excessive, too rich for films. For the main theme of *A Fistful of Dollars* I played an old Gypsy piece for Sergio which I had arranged years before for a television program, accompanying it with whip lashes, whistles and anvils... He told me to leave it almost unchanged. Sometimes Sergio takes a devilish pleasure in re-evaluating certain themes that other directors have discarded, knowing that the musical discourse is different from movie to movie. I had written the melody for the trumpet piece of the finale for a black singer in a television version of O'Neill's sea plays. Sergio told me to add the trumpet with a Mexican accompaniment of the "Deguello" type – which I really do not like – because Sergio and Cinquini had edited the images precisely on Tiomkin's "Deguello" in *Rio Bravo*. In the second picture, I had to use the trumpet again, though with guitar and carillon; in the third picture, with other things; and in the fourth we finally almost freed ourselves of it.

After the first picture I did the music before the shooting began. Sergio generally does not even give me the script: he tells me the story, the way he feels the characters, even the way the shots are composed. And I bring him the music. We talk it over and influence each other, something like a marriage where two become one flesh. Sometimes he plays the music on the set. In *Once Upon a Time in the West* it seems that this was very helpful to the actors' sense of character.

The use of the organ in *For a Few Dollars More* suggested itself to me by the fact that Volonté had his hide-out in a church and, in particular, by an almost Michelangelo-like shot of Volonté. I did not want to use just any organ music, and so I used the opening of Bach's *Fugue in D minor*. The trumpet theme starts by taking the A-G-A of the organ. My carillon is a deformation of the tenuous sound of the music box incorporated in Lee Van Cleef's watch. As in the case of the harmonica of *Once Upon a Time in the West,* we are dealing here, to use Sergio Miceli's words, with interior music, music that is born within the scene.

The voice of Edda dell'Orso had already been used in *For a Few Dollars More* . In *Once Upon a Time in the West* it becomes the protagonist. It is the human voice used like an instrument. The music for *Once Upon a Time in the West* was already composed and recorded before the shooting began. I believe that Sergio regulated the speed of the crane shot when Claudia Cardinale leaves the station, to fit the musical crescendo. The Cheyenne theme came to me almost out of the blue. We were in the recording studio, I sat down to play the piano, Sergio liked it; and so I wrote it.

In *Duck! You Sucker*, the sweet music that accompanies the collapse of the bridge expresses the dynamiter's nostalgia for his youth. The roar puts an end to his Irish memories. For the march of the beggars, since I had injected some rather vulgar things – there was even some belching (the illogical thing was to put full-stomach sounds into a march of starving men) – it seemed only right to add something more refined, like Mozart.

There is a special satisfaction in working with someone like Leone. Not only does he make excellent films, but he respects the work of the composer and the orchestra. Other directors do a bad job of mixing the music, they keep it too soft or cover it with noises. But Sergio always gave full value to what I wrote for him.

Tonino Valerii

A Pistol for Harlequin

One afternoon in 1963 Enzo Barboni (the future E.B. Clucher) and Stelvio Massi ran into Sergio Leone as they were leaving the Cinema Arlecchino in Rome. They had just seen Kurosawa's *Yojimbo* and they told him it could be made into a good Western.

Leone, who was preparing the epic *Le aquile di Roma* [The eagles of Rome], realized that it was a good suggestion and spoke about it with Franco Palaggi, known as Checco, and he in turn proposed it to Papi and Colombo of Jolly Film. Jolly had a Western of Mario Caiano's in the works, *Le pistole non discutono* (with a script by Castellano and Pipolo inspired by *The Fascist* which they had written years before for Luciano Salce). A Western from *Yojimbo* could be produced as a *recupero,* which is to say, using the same sets, costumes, and even perhaps the same actors as the other movie.

To write the script, Palaggi called on Duccio Tessari who was going through a bad period financially. The producers did not want Leone as the director – they had no great opinion of him – but Palaggi managed to convince them.

The set designer was to be the same one as in Caiano's picture, Alberto Roccianti. One day the architect Carlo Simi, who was renovating producer Colombo's apartment, passed by the Jolly offices. He saw a drawing of the set on Leone's desk and said sarcastically: "And this is supposed to be a Mexican interior?" "Why?" Leone replied, "would you be able to do better?" Without bothering to reply, Simi picked up a pencil and immediately sketched a room with a high ceiling supported by enormous wooden beams and robust trusses.

Leone was struck dumb and immediately had him taken on in place of Roccianti. Simi was to do the sets for all Leone's films.

Another clever move was to replace Franco Lavagnino with Ennio Morricone after hearing two of his motifs that Caiano had rejected for *Le pistole non discutono.*

The only one who did not lose his job was Massimo Dallamano, the director of photography. He was the first one to understand that the new P2 (two perforations) Technicolor format required a new kind of close-up that took in the face from the chin to the lower part of the forehead in order not to lose too much small detail. Furthermore Dallamano was very good at finding the proper angle quickly.

Another precious collaborator was Franco Giraldi, the underrated second-unit director. He shot the most beautiful sequence in the whole film: the Rio Bravo massacre. (Leone only shot the close-ups of Clint Eastwood.) And to think that Leone complained to me that Giraldi had ruined the movie! Gratitude is not one of his strengths.

Leone wanted James Coburn in the main role, but he was too expensive. The producers wanted to give him Cameron Mitchell, the lead in Caiano's movie, but Leone would not hear

Jean Martin and Henry Fonda in **My Name is Nobody** *directed by Tonino Valerii and produced by Sergio Leone.*

of it. One day a beautiful girl, Claudia Sartori, happened to come by. She worked in a casting agency, the William Morris, if I remember rightly. She said that she had received a 16mm copy of an episode of the Western serial *Rawhide* from America. It seemed to her that there was a young actor in it, tall and loose-limbed, who might be right for Leone.

Leone saw the film and accepted with some reluctance; to the point that he sent Mario Caiano to meet the actor at the airport. Clint Eastwood got off the plane with a small suitcase containing a poncho, hat, leather wristbands and pistol grips. Leone added the Tuscan cigar (*Virginia* actually, but Tuscans also were made to do) and, in the Italian version, the unbearable voice of Enrico Maria Salerno).

The editor was Roberto Cinquini, the excellent editor of Germi's movies. The famous sequence of the massacre of the Baxters with all those close-ups of Mexican faces laughing as they shoot, is his work. Cinquini also had the rejected shots printed and had many good shots duplicated. He was a master in this. He knew how to use the same shots as many as four or five times always starting from a different point. The dialogue is partly mine. Leone returned from Spain without the shooting script, which he had lost. I used the original script changing many things, also because during the editing, the story was modified.

With all of this I don't want to belittle Leone's merits as a director. He had worked a long time with the Americans, learning precious secrets. First shoot a master of every scene, then the details from every camera angle and with various lenses. Move from one scene to another with an indirect linking shot. Make up for the insufficiencies in the acting by characterizing the personages by their style of dressing, their tics, and using extreme close-ups, details of the eyes and other parts of the anatomy. A good editor will always be able to make something decent out of all this. It is the principle of the silent film directors who at the end of a scene left it to the cameraman to shoot a curtain blowing in the breeze, a grandfather clock ticking away, the remains of a banquet table, footsteps in the sand...

The movie premiered in Florence on a Friday in August without much publicity. For the first few days the theater was almost empty. The commercial manager of Jolly Unidis Pictures, Renato Bozza, bought dozens of tickets every day to keep the theater manager from discontinuing the run. On Monday the miracle occurred: the theater magically filled up with spectators. It was the beginning of success. A detail that

should not be forgotten is that this theater, situated near the train station, had a great many traveling salesman among its customers.

But the picture also ran into some unpleasant episodes during its career – for example, a trial for plagiarism. Leone's lawyers advised a defence based on the fact that the double-crossing hero had been inspired by a figure in a western literary work and so, if anything, Kurosawa was the plagiarist. I was given the job of discovering this work. I happened to see the announcement of a performance of *Harlequin, Servant of Two Masters* by Carlo Goldoni. I phoned Gastaldi, the fortunate owner of the *Dizionario Bompiani delle opere e dei personaggi* [Bompiani Dictionary of Literary Works and Characters], and asked him to read me the plot. That same afternoon I took the idea to Papi, feeling a little ashamed for the irreverent juxtaposition. It was passed on to the lawyers who were enthusiastic. I was given a bonus of 300,000 lire. And so it was that Goldoni became the inspiration of the Italian Western.

Leone's relations with the producers turned sour due to the success of the picture. Papi and Colombo refused to pay him his established percentage because the Spanish co-producer, whom Leone had recommended, had not even paid for the rental of the village where the movie was shot: Pedrizia di Colmenar Viejo (the stone quarry of the old beehive) fifty kilometers outside Madrid.

So, for his next movie Leone was on the outlook for a producer. He found one in the person of the attorney Alberto Grimaldi who until then had only produced a few Spanish Westerns and was looking for his big chance. Grimaldi offered Leone a blank check – so, at least, the legend goes – but he refused it in gentlemanly fashion, making do with a percentage.

A subject had to be found. A story written by Enzo dell'Aquila and another young unknown found its way onto Grimaldi's desk. It was bought at a relatively high price on the condition that the two youths renounce appearing in the credits. Maybe Leone was too much of a snob to shoot a movie whose subject had been written by two unknowns. Leone and Vincenzoni wrote the script.

The part of the bounty hunter was meant for Clint Eastwood, but Papi and Colombo were plotting to get him away from Leone. It was necessary to fly to the United States and thwart the competition. But Leone, who hadn't yet gotten rich, did not know that money bestows immortality. He was afraid of flying! I remember the atmosphere of last goodbyes that hovered in the air at that departure from Fiumicino.

Henry Fonda and the wild horde charging to the theme of The Ride of the Walkyries *in* My Name is Nobody.

Furthermore, I too for a long time had been afraid of flying. And I hadn't become either rich nor immortal. Work on the film proceeded with enthusiasm. It was one of the best troupes that Leone had ever had. I was assistant director with the job of supervising the choice of the supporting actors and preparing the sets. This was a delicate business considering that the shooting made the rounds of Rome, Madrid, Guadix, Almeria and Pedrizia di Colmenar Viejo. For example, the prison in which Volonté was kept had its exterior at Almeria, several interiors in Rome, and some in various other locations.

Regarding Volonté, the character he played was my invention. In the subject there was a baddie, Tombstone, but he was not on as high a level as the other two heroes. Leone asked me to come up with some ideas to develop this character and I suggested making him a drugged half-breed who killed under the effects of marijuana.

The following year I made my directorial debut with *Per il gusto di uccidere* [For the taste to kill], after which I made various other films, some Westerns and some not. In 1972 I was working for Leone again on *My Name Is Nobody*, which he produced and I directed.

Leone had particular reasons for wanting to produce it. Enzo Barboni's movies *(They Call Me Trinity* and *Trinity Is Still My Name)* had had unexpected international success, pushing Leone off his throne as the master of the Italian Western. Furthermore they were tongue-in-cheek parodies on the clichés of this genre. So Leone was planning artistic vengeance. Terence Hill, having ridiculed the Italian Western, would have to pay with an eye for an eye by playing straight man to one of the Western's most mythical interpreters, Henry Fonda, and so learn to recognize his own insignificance (thus the meaning of the title – *My Name Is Nobody* – which was originally supposed to be the name of a Western inspired by Ulysses' adventure with Polyphemus). In short, it was supposed to be a kind of execution of the figure of Trinity. But to get Terence Hill, Leone had to introduce many comic scenes of the kind used in the Trinity films. I was called in after he had rejected several other directors. Perhaps he chose me because, having been his assistant, he thought I would make the movie the way he wanted.

At first I refused. I had liked the script, but I was convinced that the true hero of the picture had to be Henry Fonda and not Terence Hill, as Leone maintained. In the end, several months later, I accepted, to make Fulvio Morsella, Leone's brother-in-law, happy. Leone behaved magnificently. He

accepted my version and renounced all vindictive feelings towards Trinity, who became a good kid dreaming of meeting his childhood hero. When he finally meets him, he is in trouble and Trinity helps to bring his career to a good end. I made endless on-the-spot inspections of locations in Arizona, New Mexico, Louisiana and New England. Meticulous care was taken in choosing the locations, actors and the team. The nine weeks of shooting in the United States went as smooth as silk if you ignore some friction between me and the cameraman, Nannuzzi, who tried to influence the directing without having the ability.

During the last five days of our stay in the United States, as we were shooting the finale, Leone arrived to tell me that in Madrid I would find a different cameraman and troupe. He watched the shooting and then left again. In Madrid the sets weren't ready and the costumes hadn't arrived. We had to interrupt our work for a week, and since Fonda was due to begin shooting *Ash Wednesday* immediately afterwards, Leone offered to direct the second unit with Terence Hill – who was literally dying to be directed by the master – in the sequence of the duel of the glasses in the saloon and in the village fiesta. Mancini, the organizer, warned me: "If you let Leone shoot just one frame, everyone will say he directed the picture." I did not take him seriously. Most particularly, I did not want to involve Leone in the financial damages of a delay in completing the shooting. In the end it went just the way Mancini had predicted. When the film came out many critics said Leone was the true director and I only a kind of amanuensis. And Steven Spielberg called *My Name Is Nobody* Sergio Leone's masterpiece!

Luciano Vincenzoni

Twenty Years Later

I have known Sergio since my first jobs in the field of motion pictures. The first subject I ever sold, in 1954 when I was twenty-five, was *Hanno rubato un tram* [They've stolen a streetcar]. Aldo Fabrizi bought it, and it was directed by Mario Bonnard. Leone was the assistant director; and since Bonnard was old and ill, I got the impression that Leone directed half of the movie. I remember him at Gigi Fazi's restaurant, seated at a table, silent and attentive, with Bonnard, Fabrizi and the screenwriter Maccari. Possibly, bored in the company of these old men, he would have preferred to have been out with a girl, but he stayed there since it was his job. As a young man he must have suffered boredom and humiliations, but they helped build his character, his capacity to get what he was after.

I got along well with Sergio because the Western was also my private mythology. I had only just been to see *A Fistful of Dollars* and was thinking how much I would like to write a Western when Sergio came and asked me to write the script of *For a Few Dollars More.* The subject and treatment were by Leone and his brother-in-law Fulvio Morsella. The first scene he told me about in order to work up my appetite for doing the script was the duel between Clint Eastwood and Lee Van Cleef when they stomp on each other's feet and riddle each other's hats with holes. I felt at a loss: okay, it was clearly meant to be ironic, but I couldn't imagine John Wayne stepping on Henry Fonda's foot; it would not make me laugh and would strike me as infantile. But when Sergio described the scene to me, I was convinced. After all, it was a game between aggressive children and could easily be applied to such instinctive characters. He maintained that the Western owed its success to the fact that the swaggering of the Western hero, Richard Widmark or John Wayne, was identical to that of the Roman slum kid or Trastevere roughneck. He had grown up in Trastevere and had played with these arrogant bullies who may stomp on your foot to challenge you, and he transferred these adolescent memories to the West.

This ironic quality was what most struck Americans. The film was a tremendous success. The ticket sales broke box-office records three times at the Supercinema theater. I personally handled the sales abroad. I phoned to my friend, Ilya Lopert, the vice-president of United Artists in Paris, who came to Rome with his whole staff. I took them to the Supercinema. Fortunately it was one of the record-breaking days and there were three thousand people in the theater. They saw the film in a joyous uproar of laughs and applause and they wanted to go straight to the Grand Hotel to sign the contract. They paid a guaranteed minimum that was three times the amount of the producers' rosiest hopes. In the way Americans do, as soon as the contract was signed they said: "And now let's "cross-collateralize," counterbalance profits and losses with the next picture; what is the next one going to be?" We had no project. With the tacit consent of Leone and Grimaldi I began to improvise: "A picture about three rogues running after a treasure in the midst of the Civil War, a little in the spirit of *The Great War* which you distributed in the United States."

And they immediately replied: "We'll buy it – what will it cost?" without a written script, just on our word.

In the United States even today, *For a Few Dollars More* and *The Good, the Bad and the Ugly* are shown by at least four hundred television stations a month. Leone's movies are practically the only Italian Westerns that have been successful in America. No one has seen the others; they have been handed over to television where they are broadcast maybe at night just to have something to justify showing the commercials. If Leone's films fly at 90,000 feet attitude, the others are moles that travel underground.

Then there was a cooling off in my relations with Leone and I accepted offers for two other movies, Corbucci's *A Professional Gun* and Petroni's *Death Rides a Horse,* because I earned twice as much and didn't have to argue with the directors. But it was a mistake; I would have done better to write the script for *Once Upon a Time in the West.* If I won a certain popularity in America it was not for the films of Monicelli, or Germi, or Lizzani, but precisely for Leone's Westerns; for Spielberg, Lucas, Coppola, all hold him in great esteem. Unfortunately they are less familiar with Germi.

Later we were reunited for *Duck! You Sucker.* The subject was not terribly original, but Leone managed to endow it with a certain magnitude. The difference between this film and *A Professional Gun* was also a question of the means and actors at our disposal. It is one thing to have Tony Musante and Franco Nero and quite another to work with James Coburn and Rod Steiger. The carriage that appears at the beginning of the picture was a masterpiece of carpentry with original Louis Vuitton suitcases from the end of the 1800s and a toilet like in a sleeping car. Leone wanted it to be extremely luxurious in order to emphasize all the more the humiliation of the peon. And to satisfy him they had it made. It took twelve horses to pull it; it cost a fortune. But he was right, because on the screen this carriage is important.

The idea of Rod Steiger peeing at the beginning of the movie was Sergio's. It was a game he played as a kid. In the spring he and his friends went beneath the trees where there were termite colonies and played at who could hit more of them by peeing. *Viale Glorioso* [Glorioso Street], a film subject that was never made, begins like that, with children who go to the top of some steps, pee and then run to the bottom to see which one's pee gets there first.

Another bit that Sergio was very set on was the scene where Rod Steiger slips into the cattle car, seats himself under a

birdcage and then at a certain point the little bird craps on his head. He looks up at it and comments: "And to think that for gentlemen it sings."

Sergio can be heavy-handed and exaggerated as in some fight scenes and executions, but he is never dreary. Others are dreary because they are so by nature or because they bow to the demands of the producer. If a producer says he can only allow two days for a scene and Sergio knows it will take six, he asks for eight. Another director would accept doing it in a day and a half.

Leone is capable of running over the work schedule by as many as twenty weeks, which means six billion lire, and of shooting a million and a half feet of film when what is seen on the screen is only 13,500 feet. Anyone who is capable of getting away with all of that, is very good indeed. And then he finds himself with all this beautiful footage and doesn't want to throw anything away; each frame is like a child. In fact, with *Once Upon a Time in America* he started out making one film and ended up with two: this may be the producer's salvation. If poor Michelangelo had been given a block of stone and told to sculpt the *Pietà* and a pair of Siamese Madonnas was produced, he had gotten it all wrong. But in the cinema they are cut and sold separately.

Leone's charisma allows him to make the film when and how he wants to. He is a man capable of waiting eleven years before making *Once Upon a Time in America*, a man who will not stoop to compromises – this is his strength. And he is absolutely right in this: six months later it will not interest anyone to know how many feet of film were shot, but the picture will remain in the film libraries. What counts is the result.

Leone is a trained professional with few peers; someone who personally involves himself in everything from the narrative

line to the face of the least important extra being photographed in long shot. He even knows the little differences made in the Colt Navys year by year, and set great store by these things even if no viewer could ever notice them. During the story conferences he put on a cartridge belt and spun a pistol on his finger like a cowboy. You needed to see how lovingly he touched these arms, as if they were jewels. He is a man who loves objects, someone who collects eighteenth century Roman silver, furniture, pictures. He has great knowledge of visual things. He is one of those rare directors for whom you may write a scene with a potential of ten and you get it back from him with a potential of a hundred. And when you see the picture, you ask yourself: "By God, did I really write that?" In *The Good, the Bad and the Ugly* there is an amusing exchange of quips between the two leads sitting around a fire. Sergio had postponed shooting this scene for several days while his assistants were looking for a location along a mountain path with a majestic background that would give the dialogue its full impact.

Let's take the opening of *Once Upon a Time in the West*: here, Leone's memory for movies came into play. He recalled *High Noon* with the three killers dying of boredom in the station; and he added his grandiose eye for a scene. He had hundreds – thousands – of railroad ties brought over to construct the platform where Bronson confronts the three killers. It is a great visual idea. Another director would have said: "We already have the grass, the boulders... isn't it the same thing?" Or then, that immense drugstore situated in the midst of the desert. Leone did not care if it was believable, he cared about the depth it gave to the scene.

There was already talk of the sets for *Once Upon a Time in America*. He had an opium den made as big as a train station with clouds of smoke and bunk beds... it was an exaggeration because real opium dens in the Chinese quarter are rather pathetic little places. But the little man seated below the gigantic screen in a movie theater looks up at a head measuring twelve by six feet. These images overwhelm him and when he leaves he takes away a lasting impression. For Leone it is necessary to *épater*... always.

After having worked with many directors who were real charlatans, I realized Sergio's great qualities for, he is a person who believes in what he does. Westerns can make a comeback because a new public is growing up. Those who are tired of Westerns are forty by now and they do not go to pictures anymore; it is their children who do, and they are eighteen.

There are students at UCLA who have seen our movies as many as ten times.

I have written the treatment for a *The Good, the Bad and the Ugly – 2,* and it would only require Sergio's say-so to make it. It begins twenty years after the end of the first: one stormy evening in a village on the edge of nowhere a dust-covered horseman arrives. He enters the deserted saloon, the bartender pours him a drink and this sand-bleached spectre – it is Eli Wallach – asks: "Have you seen a blond son-of-a-bitch with a cigar? I've been looking for him for twenty years." The answer is *no.* He leaves. The wind creates swirls of straw, a page from a newspaper flies up into his face. On it is a photograph of Clint Eastwood graying a little, with the caption: "Next week our mayor is marrying Miss What's-her-name thus culminating a long dream of love." Exulted, Wallach turns to his horse saying: "We've found him!" and the horse dies from the strain of the emotion. Wallach steals another horse and gallops off. Blowing around the town square, the newspaper is trapped by a booted foot and is grasped by a hand: it is Lee Van Cleef's, the twin brother of the villain who died in the first movie, intent on revenge.

We are in Clint Eastwood's town. Black-framed posters mourn the death of the mayor killed in a cowardly ambush. Wallach is terribly disappointed. He goes to the cemetery where he finds the grave with a cross, the poncho, the sombrero and a lighted cigar on an iron brace. Beside the grave stands a tall blond kid, Clint Eastwood's son, talking to the dead man: "As you ordered me to do, I have sold the land and the herds and I've raised $220,000. I am going East to invest it all in the railroads. I'll be back to visit you soon. Someone will come to change your cigar every day." He starts to leave when he hears a voice from the grave: "Watch out, kid, the world is full of sons-of-bitches." Wallach follows the boy and from behind a tombstone Lee Van Cleef's hawk-like nose peeks out.

Great adventures, chases, surprise actions. Lee Van Cleef overtakes Clint Eastwood's son in the desert, steals his money, makes him undress, ties him up, and smears him with honey while columns of ants approach, as in a classic with Wallace Berry. Providentially a strange nun arrives leading a caravan of girls who put on religious shows. He also runs into Eli Wallach, and the two of them go off to hunt down Lee Van Cleef. They happen upon a village surrounded by the army; Lee Van Cleef and his brigands are holed up in a school house with some hostages, including the little nun. The two friends offer themselves as substitute hostages, while in fact they are only thinking of getting the money back.

They succeed in this, kill Lee Van Cleef, and recover the money. Eli Wallach proposes splitting it between them, but the door opens, the soldiers enter and Clint Eastwood's son shows them the notice of the reward on Eli Wallach's head. Wallach is taken into the square to be hanged. His neck is already in the noose when a shot is fired from a nearby hill that cuts the noose down and Wallach manages to escape.

Clint Eastwood has agreed to lend his voice and even to produce the movie. An American producer has come to Rome and offered a million dollars for it. Leone would not even have to direct it – the director would be a young American, Joe Dante – but for the moment Leone has refused to give his okay. Who knows why?

These testimonies were recorded on tape by the author in 1983 and 1984. The text by Peter Bogdanovich is a partial translation of an article published in the November 26, 1973 issue of *New York.*

Sergio Leone (second from the left) and Aldo Fabrizi in the days of **Hanno rubato un tram.**

Sergio Leone *during the shooting of*
Once Upon a Time in America.

Filmography

1945-1959

Leone works as assistant director in the making of about fifty films, among which: *The Bicycle Thief* (Vittorio De Sica, 1948), *La leggenda di Faust* and *Il trovatore* (Carmine Gallone, 1949), *Fabiola* (Alessandro Blasetti, 1949), *La forza del destino* (Carmine Gallone, 1950), *Il brigante Musolino* (Mario Camerini, 1950), *Quo Vadis?* (Mervyn Le Roy, 1951), *I tre corsari* and *Iolanda, la figlia del corsaro nero* (Mario Soldati, 1952), *La tratta delle bianche* (Mario Camerini, 1952), *Helen of Troy* (Robert Wise and, uncredited, Raoul Walsh, 1953), *L'uomo, la bestia e la virtù* (Steno, 1953), *La marsina stretta,* an episode in *Questa è la vita* (Aldo Fabrizi, 1954), *Tradita* (Mario Bonnard, 1954), *Hanno rubato un tram* (Mario Bonnard, 1955), *Ben Hur* (William Wyler, 1958), *The Nun's Story,* (Fred Zinnemann, 1958). He collaborates on the script of *Nel segno di Roma* (Guido Brignone and, uncredited, Riccardo Freda and Michelangelo Antonioni, 1958) and *Afrodite, la dea dell'amore* (Mario Bonnard, 1958).

1959

Last Days of Pompeii (Gli ultimi giorni di Pompei)
Les derniers jours de Pompei
Director: Sergio Leone (the credits name Mario Bonnard as director and Leone as second-unit director); *Production:* Cinemaproduzioni Associate (Rome), Procusa (Madrid), Transocean (Munich); *Distribution:* Filmar and (after 1976) Fida; in the USA: United Artists; *Story:* Based on a novel by Bulwer Lytton; *Screenplay:* Ennio De Concini, Luigi Emmanuelli, Sergio Corbucci, Sergio Leone, Duccio Tessari; *Photography:* Antonio Ballestreros (Totalscope-Eastmancolor; *Color consultant:* Jorge Grau; *Sets:* Ramiro Gomez; *Costumes:* Vittorio Rossi; *Editing:* Eraldo da Roma; *Music:* Angelo Francesco Lavagnino; *Second-unit director:* Duccio Tessari; *Assistant director:* Sergio Corbucci; *Photography assistant:* Enzo Barboni; *Cast:* Steve Reeves, Christine Kaufmann, Fernando Rey, Barbara Carroll, Anne Marie Baumann, Mino Doro, Carlo Tamberlani, Guillermo Marin, Angel Aranda, Mimmo Palmara, Mario Berriatua, Mario Morales, Ignazio Dolce, Antonio Casas, Tony Richards, Angel Ortiz, Lola Torres; *Length:* 100 minutes (American version: 103 minutes).

1960

The Colossus of Rhodes (Il colosso di Rodi)
Le Colosse de Rhodes
El coloso de Rhodas
Director: Sergio Leone; *Production:* Cineproduzioni associate (Rome), Procusa (Madrid), Comptoir Français, Ciné Télévision (Paris); *Acting producer:* Michele Scaglione; *Distribution:* Filmar, and (after 1977) Pac, in the USA: MGM; *Screenplay:* Luciano Chitarrini, Ennio De Concini, Carlo Gualtieri, Sergio Leone, Luciano Martino, Aggeo Savioli, Cesare Seccia, Duccio Tessari; *Photography:* Antonio Ballestreros, Emilio Foriscot (Eastmancolor, Supertotalscope); *Sets:* Ramiro Gomez; *Costumes:* Vittorio Rossi; *Music:* Angelo Francesco Lavagnino; *Editing:* Eraldo da Roma;

Special effects: Vittorio Galliano, Eros Baciucchi; *Second-unit director:* Jorge Grau; *Assistant director:* Michele Lupo; *Cast:* Rory Calhoun (Darius), Lea Massari (Diala), George Marchal (Peliocles), Mabel Karr (Mirte), Angel Aranda (Koros), Mimmo Palmara (Ares), Roberto Camardiel (Xerxes), Jorge Rigaud (Lissipus), Carlo Tamberlani (Xenon), Conrado San Martin (Tireus), Alf Randall [Alfio Caltabiano] (Creontes), José Suarez, Felix Fernandez (Caretes), Antonio Casas (Phoenician ambassador), Fernando Calzado, José Vilches, Arturo Cabre, Angel Menendez, Yan Larrar; *Length:* 142 minutes.

1961-1963

Collaborates on the scripts of *Duel of Titans (Romolo e Remo)* (Sergio Corbucci, 1961) and *Le sette sfide* (Primo Zeglio, 1961). Second-unit director of *Sodom and Gomorrah* (Robert Aldrich, 1961-1962). Shoots the battle scenes near Marrakech in two weeks with 1,000 horsemen (in the credits Leone appears as co-director).

1964

A Fistful of Dollars (Per un pugno di dollari)
Pour une poignée de dollars
Por un puñado de dólares
Director: Bob Robertson [Sergio Leone]; *Production:* Jolly Film (Rome), Ocean Produktion, Constantin Film (Munich); *Distribution:* Unidis, USA: United Artists; *Story:* based on *Yojimbo* (Akira Kurosawa, 1961); *Screenplay:* Sergio Leone, Duccio Tessari, Victor A. Catena, G. Schock; *Photography:* Jack Dalmas [Massimo Dallamano], Federico Larraya (Technicolor, Techniscope); *Music:* Dan Savio [Ennio Morricone]; *Sets and Costumes:* Charles Simons [Carlo Simi]; *Editing:* Bob Quintle [Roberto Cinquini]; *Second-unit director:* Frank Prestland [Franco Giraldi]; *Cast:* Clint Eastwood (Joe), John Wells [Gian Maria Volonté] (Ramon Rojo), Marianne Koch (Marisol), Josè «Pepe» Calvo (Silvanito), Wolfgang Lukschy (John Baxter), Sieghardt Rupp (Esteban Rojo), Antonio Prieto (Benito Rojo), Margarita Lozano (Consuelo Baxter), Josef Egger (Piripero), Daniel Martin (Julian), Benny Reeves [Benito Stefanelli] (Rubio), Richard Stuyvesant [Mario Brega] (Chico), Carol Brown [Bruno Carotenuto] (Antonio Baxter), Antonio Vico, Raf Baldassarre, Aldo Sambrell, Umberto Spadaro, the little Fredy Arco (Jesus); *Length:* 100 minutes (French version: 95 minutes; American version: 96 minutes); *Location shots:* La Pedrizia di Colmenar Viejo (Madrid).

1965

For a Few Dollars More (Per qualche dollaro in più)
Et pour quelques dollars de plus
La muerte tenia un precio
Director: Sergio Leone; *Production:* Alberto Grimaldi for Pea (Rome), Constantin Film (Munich), Arturo Gonzales (Madrid); *Distribution:* Pea,

in the USA: United Artists; *Story:* Sergio Leone, Fulvio Morsella; *Screenplay:* Sergio Leone, Luciano Vincenzoni; *Photography:* Massimo Dallamano (Technicolor, Techniscope); *Cameraman:* Aldo Ricci; *Sets:* Carlo Simi; *Editing:* Eugenio Alabiso, Giorgio Serralonga; *Music:* Ennio Morricone; *Musical direction:* Bruno Nicolai; *Assistant directors:* Tonino Valerii, Fernando di Leo; *Cast:* Clint Eastwood (Monko), Lee Van Cleef (Colonel Douglas Mortimer), Gian Maria Volonté (El Indio), Rosemarie Dexter (the Colonel's sister), Klaus Kinski (Wild, the hunchback), Josef Egger ("the prophet"), Luigi Pistilli (Groggy), Mario Brega (Nino), Mara Krupp (wife of the inn proprietor), Panos Papadopoulos, Benito Stefanelli, Roberto Camardiel, Aldo Sambrell, Luis Rodriguez, Diana Rabito, Giovanni Tarallo, Mario Meniconi, Lorenzo Robledo, Tomas Blanco, Sergio Mendizabal, Dante Maggio; *Length:* 130 minutes; *Location shots:* Almeria, Guadix, Madrid.

1966
The Good, the Bad and the Ugly / Two Magnificent Rogues (Il buono, il brutto, il cattivo)
Le Bon, la brute et le truand
El bueno, el feo y el malo
Director: Sergio Leone, *Production:* Alberto Grimaldi for Pea; *Distribution:* Pea, USA: United Artists; *Story:* Sergio Leone, Luciano Vincenzoni; *Screenplay:* Sergio Leone, Luciano Vincenzoni, Age-Scarpelli; *Photography:* Tonino Delli Colli (Technicolor, Techniscope); *Music:* Ennio Morricone; *Musical direction:* Bruno Nicolai; *Sets:* Carlo Simi; *Editing:* Nino Baragli; *Special effects:* Eros Baciucchi; *Cast:* Clint Eastwood (the Good, Blondie), Eli Wallach (the Ugly, Tuco), Lee Van Cleef (the Bad, Angel Eyes), Aldo Giuffré (a nothern officer), Mario Brega (Caporal Wallace), Luigi Pistilli (Father Ramirez), Al Mulloch (one-armed gunman), Rada Rassimov (Maria, the prostitute), Angelo Novi (a monk), Enzo Petito, Claudio and Sandro Sarchilli, Chelo Alonso (Mexican peons), Silvana Bacci, Claudio Stefanelli, Livio Lorenzon (Baker), Antonio Casas, John Janos Bartha, Sergio Mendizibal, Lorenzo Robledo; *Length:* 182 minutes (French version: 166 minutes; American version: 161 minutes); *Location shots:* Almeria, Burgos.

1968
Once Upon a Time in the West (C'era una volta il West)
Il était une fois dans l'Ouest
Hasta que llegò su hora
Director: Sergio Leone; *Production:* Bino Cicogna for Rafran Cinematografica, San Marco Films; *Distribution:* Euro, in the USA: Paramount; *Story:* Dario Argento, Bernardo Bertolucci, Sergio Leone; *Screenplay:* Sergio Donati, Sergio Leone; *Photography:* Tonino Delli Colli (Technicolor, Techniscope); *Sets and Costumes:* Carlo Simi; *Decorative artist:* Carlo Leva; *Sound:* Claudio Maielli; *Editing:* Nino Baragli; *Music and musical direction:* Ennio Morricone; *Make-up:* Alberto De Rossi; *Assistant director:* Giancarlo Santi; *Cast:* Henry Fonda (Frank), Claudia Cardinale (Jill McBain), Charles Bronson (Harmonica), Jason Robards (Cheyenne), Gabriele Ferzetti (Morton), Frank Wolff (Brett McBain), Keenan Wynn (the sheriff), Paolo Stoppa (Sam), Marco Zuanelli (Wobbles), Lionel Stander (the proprietor of the tavern), Jack Elam (Snaky), Al Mulloch (Knuckles), Woody Strode (Stony), John Frederick (Frank's man), Dino Mele (Harmonica young), Enzo Santaniello (Timmy McBain), Benito

Stefanelli, Livio Andronico, Salvo Basile, Claudio Mancini (Harmonica's elder brother), Aldo Berti, Marilù Carteny, Luigi Ciavarro, Spartaco Conversi, Renato Pinciroli, Ivan G. Scratuglia, Corrado San Martin; *Length:* 167 minutes (American version: 165 minutes; French version: 164 minutes; English version: 155 minutes; Restored edition: 181 minutes); *Location shots:* Utah, Arizona, Almeria, Guadix.

1970
Together with Nanni Loy, Elio Petri, Luchino Visconti and others, Leone endorses a "counter-information" movie *12 dicembre* or *Document on Giuseppe Pinelli on the Piazza Fontana Massacre.*

1971
Duck! You Sucker (Giù la testa)
Il était une fois la révolution
A Fistful of Dynamite
Agáchate, maldito
Director: Sergio Leone; *Production:* Fulvio Morsella for Rafran Cinematografica, San Marco Films, Miura; *Distribution:* Euro, in the USA: United Artists; *Story:* Sergio Donati, Sergio Leone; *Screenplay:* Sergio Donati, Sergio Leone, Luciano Vincenzoni; *Photography:* Giuseppe Ruzzolini (Technicolor, Techniscope); *Sets:* Andrea Grisanti; *Decorative artist:* Dario Micheli; *Costumes:* Franco Carretti; *Music and musical direction:* Ennio Morricone; *Editing:* Nino Baragli; *Second-unit photography:* Franco Delli Colli; *Fencing master:* Benito Stefanelli; *Special effects:* Antonio Margheriti; *Cast:* Rod Steiger (Juan Miranda), James Coburn (John-Sean Mallory), Romolo Valli (Doctor Villega), Franco Graziosi (Don Jaime, the Governor), Domingo Antoine (Colonel Gutierrez, Gunther Reza), Rick Battaglia (Santerna), Maria Monti (Adelita), Goffredo Pistoni (Nino), Roy Bosier (the landowner), Antonio Casal (notary), John Frederick (the American), Jean Rougeul (priest), Corrado Solari (Sebastian), Renato Pontecchi (Pepe), Franco Collace (Napoleone), Michael Harvey (a Yankee), Amelio Perlini (peon), Poldo Bendandi and Furio Meniconi (two revolutionaries, shot) Biagio la Rocca ("Benito"), Vincenzo Norvese (Pancho), Omar Bonano, Giulio Battiferri, Franco Tocci, Stefano Oppedisano, Rosita Torosh; *Length:* 154 minutes (American version and British: 138 minutes; Restored version: 160 minutes); *Location shots:* Dublin, Almeria, Grenada, Madrid.

1973-1983
During this period Leone made several television commercials, among them one for the Gervais company (*Dany Danone*), one for Talbot Motors (*Talbot Solara*) and two for Renault. In the first (*Petra*), filmed in Jordan, the birth of the Renault 18 takes place in a temple. The car comes out of the darkness, leaves the temple (with an invisible driver), descends the steps and meanders around Petra. Occasionally a goddess appears to block its path: the car blinks its headlights, a flirtation takes place. Finally the goddess lets it pass and the car drives away on the superhighway. In the second commercial (*Il diesel si scatena*) a car leaps out of control in the middle of an arena. ("They wanted me to shoot it in a marble quarry in Carrara, but I preferred the Roman arena in Tunis. It is much more impressive – it seems like the Coliseum.") The music is Ennio Morricone's. This film won the platinum Minerva, the Oscar of commercials.

1984

Once Upon a Time in America (C'era una volta in America)
Il était une fois en Amérique
Erase una vez en América
Director: Sergio Leone; *Production:* Arnon Milchan for Ladd Company; *Executive producer:* Claudio Mancini; *Distribution:* Titanus, in the USA: Warner Bros; *Story:* based on the novel *The Hoods* by Harry Grey; *Screenplay:* Leonardo Benvenuti, Piero de Bernardi, Enrico Medioli, Franco Arcalli, Franco Ferrini, Sergio Leone; *Added dialogue:* Stuart Kaminutesky; *Photography:* Tonino Delli Colli (Technicolor); *Sets:* Carlo Simi; *Costumes:* Gabriella Pescucci; *Editing:* Nino Baragli; *Music and musical direction:* Ennio Morricone; *Songs:* "God Bless America" (Berlin), "Summertime" (George and Ira Gershwin and Dubose Heyward), "Night and Day" (Porter), "Yesterday" (Lennon and McCartney), "Amapola" (La Calle) and ouverture of *La gazza ladra* (Rossini); *Casting:* Cis Corman and Joy Todd; *First assistant director:* Fabrizio Sergenti Castellani; *Cast:* Robert De Niro (Noodles), James Woods (Max), Elizabeth McGovern (Deborah); Treat Williams (Jimmy O'Donnell), Tuesday Weld (Carol), Burt Young (Joe), Joe Pesci (Frankie), Danny Aiello (Police Chief Aiello), William Forsythe (Cockeye), James Hayden (Patsy), Darlanne Fleugel (Eve), Larry Rapp (Fat Moe), Dutch Miller (Van Linden), Robert Harper (Sharkey), Richard Bright (Chicken Joe), Gerard Murphy (Crowning), Amy Rider (Peggy), Olga Karlatos (Woman in the puppet theater), Ray Dittrich (Trigger), Frank Gio (Beefy), Karen Shallo (Mrs Aiello), Angelo Florio (Willie the Ape), Scott Tiler (Young Noodles), Rusty Jacobs (Max adolescent/David), Brian Bloom (Young Patsy), Adrian Curran (Young Cockeye), Mike Monetti (Young Fat Moe), Noah Moazezi (Dominic), James Russo (Bugsy), Frankie Caserta and Joey Marzella (Bugsy's gang), Clem Caserta (Al Capuano), Frank Sisto (Fred Capuano), Jerry Strivelli (Johnny Capuano), Julie Cohen (Young Peggy), Marvin Scott (Interviewer), Mike Gendel (Irving Gold), Paul Herman (Monkey), Ann Neville (Girl in the coffin), Joey Faye (adorable old man), Mario Brega (Mandy), Linda Ipanema (Nurse Thompson), Tandy Cronin (Reporter 1), Richard Zobel (Reporter 2), Baxter Harris (Reporter 3), Arnon Milchan (Chauffeur), Bruno Iannone (Thug), Marty Licata (Cemetery caretaker), Marcia Jean Kurtz (Max's mother), Estelle Harris (Peggy's mother), Richard Forony (Whitey), Gerrit Debeer (Drunk), Jennifer Connelly (Young Deborah), Margherita Pace (Body double for Jennifer Connelly), Alexander Godfrey (Newsstand man), Cliff Cudney, Paul Farentino, Bruce Bahrenburg, Mort Freeman, Sandra Solberg, Jay Zeely, Massimo Liti; *Length:* 218 minutes; *Location shots:* New York, Montreal, St. Petersburg Beach (Florida), Paris, Venice Lido, Bellagio, Pietralata.

Productions

In addition to *Once Upon a Time in the West* and *Duck! You Sucker*, Sergio Leone produced, or co-produced, the following films:

1973

My Name Is Nobody (Il mio nome è Nessuno)
Mon nom est Personne
Mi nombre es ninguno
Director: Tonino Valerii (three of Terence Hill's scenes were directed by Sergio Leone); *Production:* Fulvio Morsella for Rafran Cinematografica (Rome), Les Films Jacques Leitienne-La Societé Alcinter (Paris), La Societé Imp. Ex. Ci. (Nice), Rialto Film Preven Philippsen (Berlin); *Distribution:* Titanus, in the USA: Universal; *Story:* Ernesto Gastaldi, Fulvio Morsella from an idea by Sergio Leone; *Photography:* Armando Nannuzzi (in the USA), Giuseppe Ruzzolini; *Cameraman:* E. Polacco; *Music composed and directed by:* Ennio Morricone; *Editing:* Nino Baragli; *Sets:* Gianni Polidori; *Costumes:* Vera Marzot; *Furnishings:* Massimo Tavazzi; *Special effects:* Giovanni Corridori; *Stunt supervisor:* Benito Stefanelli; *Assistant director:* Stefano Rolla; *Cast:* Henry Fonda (Jack Beauregard), Terence Hill [Mario Girotti] (Nobody), Jean Martin (Sullivan), Piero Lulli (the sheriff), Leo Gordon (Red), R.G. Armstrong (Honest John), Remus Peets (Big Gun), Mario Brega (Pedro), Antoine Saint Jean (Scape), Benito Stefanelli (Porteley), Mark Mazza (Don John), Franco Angrisano (train engineer), Alexander Allerson (Rex), Angelo Novi (bartender), Tommy Polgar (Juan), Carla Mancini (Mother), Antonio Luigi Guerra (an officer), Emile Feist, Geoffrey Lewis (barbers); Antonio Palombi, Neil Summers, Steve Kanaly, Humbert Mittendorf, Ulrich Muller, Claus Schmidt; *Length:* 118 minutes (American version: 115 minutes; English version: 116 minutes); *Location shots:* New Orleans, Almeria.

1975

A genius (Un genio, due compari, un pollo)
Un génie, deux associés, une cloche
Director: Damiano Damiani (Giuliano Montaldo, who is not mentioned in the credits, shot some scenes; Leone also filmed one scene); *Production:* Fulvio Morsella and Claudio Mancini for Rafran Cinematografica (Rome), Amif (Paris), Rialto film (Berlin); *Distribution:* Titanus; *Screenplay:* Ernesto Gastaldi, Fulvio Morsella, Damiano Damiani, based on a story by Ernesto Gastaldi and Fulvio Morsella; *Photography:* Giuseppe Ruzzolini (Technicolor); *Sets:* Carlo Simi and Francesco Bronzi; *Costumes:* Franco Caretti; *Music:* Ennio Morricone; *Cast:* Terence Hill [Mario Girotti], Miou-Miou, Robert Charlebois, Patrick McGoohan, Klaus Kinski, Jean Martin, Mario Brega, Raimund Harmstorf.

1977

Il gatto
Director: Luigi Comencini; *Assistant director:* Massimo Patrizi; *Production:* Sergio Leone, Romano Cardarelli for Rafran Cinematografica; *Distribution:* United Artists; *Screenplay:* Rodolfo Sonego, Augusto Caminito and Fulvio Marcolin, based on a story by Rodolfo Sonego; *Photography:* Ennio Guarnieri (color); *Music:* Ennio Morricone; *Sets:* Dante Ferretti; *Editing:* Nino Baragli: *Cast:* Ugo Tognazzi, Mariangela Melato, Michel Galabru, Jean Martin, Dalila di Lazzaro, Aldo Reggiani, Philippe Leroy, Mario Brega, Bruno Gambarotta, Luigi Comencini.

1979

Il giocattolo
Director: Giuliano Montaldo; *Production:* Claudio Mancini, Fulvio - Morsella for Rafran Cinematografica, Alex Cucchi; *Distribution:* Titanus; *Screenplay:* Sergio Donati, Nino Manfredi, Giuliano Montaldo, based on a story by Sergio Donati; *Photography:* Ennio Guarnieri (color Technospes); *Sets:* Luigi Scaccianoce; *Editing:* Nino Baragli; *Music:* Ennio Morricone; *Cast:* Nino Manfredi, Marlène Jobert, Arnoldo Foà, Olga Karlatos, Pamela Villoresi, Vittorio Mezzogiorno, Mario Brega, Daniele Formica.

1980
Un sacco bello
Director: Carlo Verdone; *Production:* Romano Cardarelli for Medusa Cinematografica; *Distribution:* Medusa; *Screenplay:* Leo Benvenuti, Piero De Bernardi, Carlo Verdone; *Photography:* Ennio Guarnieri (color Technospes); *Music:* Ennio Morricone; *Sets:* Carlo Simi; *Cast:* Carlo Verdone, Veronica Miriel, Mario Brega, Renato Scarpa.

Film Projects Never Realized

Viale Glorioso
A film of memories that takes its name from the Trastevere street where Leone spent a good part of his adolescence. Written before Fellini's *I vitelloni*, it was proposed to producers in vain after the success of Leone's first Western.

Stalingrad
An Italo-Soviet co-production, the film was to begin with a cannonade and a boy falling out of bed. The whole battle is seen through the eyes of this fourteen-year-old boy.

Vado, l'ammazzo e torno
With Marcello Mastroianni. The story of Gaetano Bresci, the anarchist who assassinated King Umberto I at Monza in July 1900.
    "He was a half-hearted anarchist who had left America to escape from a difficult family situation and who tried to vent his hatred of the world by participating in the plot against Umberto I. He was a man full of doubts, uncertainties, impulses, losses of will power – a very human personage and thus well-suited to Mastroianni's temperament." (From an interview with Angelo Lucano that appeared in *La Rivista del Cinematografo*, January 1967.)

Don Chisciotte
Sancho Panza and Don Quixote perplexed in modern America.

Cent'anni di solitudine
A television movie in ten episodes based on Gabriel Garcia Marquez's novel *One Hundred Years of Solitude*.
"Television asked me to direct *Garibaldi* and *Marco Polo* (the Chinese wanted either me or Wertmüller), but they constantly rejected Marquez."

Viaggio al termine della notte
From Céline's novel *Journey to the End of Night*. "It remains the dream of my life. But I ask myself if it weren't better left alone, all the more since I, for better or worse, am a desecrator. It's an enormous risk."

La vera storia della Monaca di Monza
(The True Story of the Nun of Monza)
From the trial documents that the Church authorities have finally made public.
"It is a great temptation for me to shoot a movie entirely within the walls of a convent. It is far from my usual subject matter, but at bottom my way

of shooting, which pays much attention to psychological states, could be suited to this kind of a story."

Leningrad
"The movie is to open with Shostakovitch composing his *Leningrad Symphony* in his room. This music is the background for a long helicopter sequence starting from Shostakovitch's house and following the crowd coming into the street armed with rifles, getting onto trams and reaching the front lines on the outskirts of the city. The camera continues moving until it reaches the line of German panzers ready to launch its attack. The idea came up in the sixties. Speaking with various intellectuals, Italian and French ones included, I became aware that they were confusing the battle of Leningrad with that of Stalingrad. So this made me want to read Harrison Salisbury's book *The Nine Hundred Days*. I was struck by these people's readiness to sacrifice their lives. In three years forty per cent of the population of Leningrad died – 1,300,000 people. In a documentary of the time, one sees the workers when the siege was announced. The camera pans their faces from which one sees that the Germans would never enter. And Hitler was counting on a blitz. He had tickets printed up for a concert of Wagner's music that was to take place at the Leningrad Philharmonic ten days after the start of the siege. There were some cruel facts too, episodes of cannibalism and scenes of women who could not manage to transport the dead because their bodies were frozen. I was moved by that little girl, a kind of Anna Frank, who made daily entries in her diary about the deaths of her relatives – her grandmother, her sister... and at the end: '...and today I have been left alone.' Only her diary was found...
"De Niro is the typical American reporter, first cynical and then more willing to become involved, like in *For Whom the Bell Tolls*. He expected to stay there a few months. Instead he stayed there forever. The woman will be a party member. We don't yet know quite what her profession should be. If they found her together with a Westerner it meant twelve years of prison for her. An American and a Russian, the two world powers that today hold the destiny of the world in their hands – and all around then the apocalypse. But with many little intertwining stories. It is no *Zhivago;* it is a difficult movie to construct. At the end he dies, a worker's death, but which we will not see directly. In a movie house they show a documentary he shot with a hand camera on the last day of the siege. Germans fleeing, the Russians pursuing, grenades coming from all sides, and then an explosion in front of the camera. The Russian woman is in the theater. She has their little girl in her arms, a few months old.
"... I can't mention Salisbury, for the Russians don't have good memories of him. Instead I have chosen a book recommended by Giulietto Chiesa, the Moscow correspondent of *L'Unità*, a book written by two Russians telling of the siege day by day.
This is Russia seen through the eyes of an American, which are almost my eyes. However I am going to do plenty of research; it will take a year to write the script, five months of which will be spent in Russia. I will write it with Arnold Yanovich Vittol who wrote a television movie on the siege, with an American – I think it will be Alvin Sargent – and two Italians, Benvenuti and De Bernardi. I hope to leave in a few days. I've been sent an article from the Leningrad *Pravda* announcing the movie." (From an interview conducted by Oreste De Fornari that appeared in *L'Europeo*, March 25, 1988.)

Bibliography

Books on Sergio Leone and on the Italian Western:

FRANCO FERRINI, *L'antiwestern e il caso Leone*, Bianco e Nero, Rome, 1971.

LAURENCE STAIG and TONY WILLIAMS, *Italian Western (The Opera of Violence)* Lorrimer, London, 1975.

GILLES LAMBERT, *Les bons, les sales, les méchants et les propres de Sergio Leone*, Solar, Paris, 1976.

MASSIMO MOSCATI, *Western all'italiana (Guida ai 407 film, ai registi e agli attori)*, Pan, Milan, 1978.

CHRISTOPHER FRAYLING, *Spaghetti Westerns (Cowboys and Europeans from Karl May to Sergio Leone)*, Routledge & Kegan Paul, London, Boston et Henley, 1981.

ALAIN PETIT, *20 ans du Western Européen* (vol. I: *Les Realisateurs*; vol. II: *Dix chefs d'œuvre du Western Européen*), Ed. by Meduse, Paris, 1981.

GIAN LHASSA, *Seul au monde dans le Western Italien* (vol. I: *Une poignée de themes*; vol. II: *Des hommes seuls*; vol. III: *Dictionnaire du Western Italien*, with the collaboration of Michel Lequeux), Ed. Grand Angle, Mariembourg (Belgium), 1983.

GILLES CÉBE, *Sergio Leone*, Henry Veyrier, Paris, 1984.

DIEGO GABUTTI, *C'era una volta in America*, Rizzoli, Milan, 1984.

ROBERT C. CUMBOW, *Once Upon a Time: The Films of Sergio Leone*, Scarecrow Press Inc., Metuchen, New Jersey, 1987.

NOËL SIMSOLO, *Conversations avec Sergio Leone*, Stock Cinéma, Paris, 1987.

MARCELLO GAROFALO, *C'era una volta in America, Photographic Memories*, Editalia, Rome, 1988.

FRANCESCO MININNI, *Sergio Leone*, Il castoro cinema, La Nuova Italia, Florence, 1989.

G. GRESSARD, *Sergio Leone*, J'ai lu, Paris, 1989.

ROBERTO PUGLIESE (edited by), *Sergio Leone*, Venezia Circuito Cinema, 1989.

CARLOS AGUILAR, *Sergio Leone*, Ediciones Catedra, Madrid, 1990.

GIANNI DI CLAUDIO, *Directed by Sergio Leone*, Libreria Universitaria Editrice, Chieti, 1990.

CLAVER SALIZZATO, CARLO COZZI (edited by), *C'era una volta*, 38° Spoleto Cinema, 1995.

ROBERTO LASAGNA, *Sergio Leone*, Ripostes, Salerno, 1996.

LUCA BEATRICE, *Al cuore Ramon, al cuore (La leggenda del western all'italiana)*, Tarab, Florence, 1996.

Selected essays and articles on Sergio Leone and his films:

MARIO SOLDATI, "Nascita del western italiano." *L'Europeo* November 28, 1964 (re-published in the anthology *Da spettatore*, Mondadori, Milan, 1973).

DOMENICO PAOLELLA, "La psicoanalisi dei poveri." *Midi-Minuit Fantastique*, n° 12, May 1965.

UGO PIRRO, "Da Caltiki a Un pugno di dollari." *Ulisse*, a. XVIII, n° 56, October 1965.

JOHN FRANCIS LANE, "La strada per Fort Alamo." *Films and Filming*, vol. II, n° 6, 1965.

ALBERTO ABRUZZESE, "Mito della violenza e pistole scariche." *Cinemasessanta*, n° 54, 1965.

GOFFREDO FOFI, "Lettre d'Italie: le western et le reste." *Positif*, n° 76, 1966.

TINO RANIERI, "Il western casalingo." *Teatro e cinema*, n° 1, January-March 1967.

ENZO NATTA, "Il buono, il brutto, il cattivo." *Cineforum*, n° 61, January 1967.

MASSIMO NEGARVILLE, "Il buono, il brutto, il cattivo." *Ombre rosse*, n° 1, May 1967.

NUCCIO LODATO and GIANNI L. DALLA VALLE, "Western all'italiana: morte presunta di un genere." *Civiltà dell'immagine*, n° 4, August 1967.

UMBERTO ROSSI, "È già iniziata la resa dei conti?" *Civiltà dell'immagine*, n° 4, August 1967.

TULLIO KEZICH, "Il western all'italiana." *Catalogo Bolaffi del cinema italiano*, Turin, 1967.

PIO BALDELLI, "Western à l'italienne." *Image et Son*, n° 206, May 1967.

SYLVIE PIERRE, "Le Bon, la Brute et le Truand." *Cahiers du cinéma*, n° 200, April-May 1968.

RAYMOND DURGNAT, "The Good, the Bad and the Ugly." *Films and Filming*, November 1968.

FERNALDO DI GIAMMATTEO, "Che guaio avere sognato la rivoluzione." *Bianco e Nero*, n°ˢ 1-2, January-February 1969.

JEAN A. GILI, "...un univers fabriqué de toutes pièces.." *Cinéma 69*, n° 140, November 1969.

MICHEL MARDORE, "Il était une fois dans l'Ouest." *Le nouvel observateur*, August 1969.

SERGE DANEY, "Il était une fois dans l'Ouest." *Cahiers du cinéma*, n° 216, October 1969.

MICHEL CIMENT, "Il était une fois dans l'Ouest." *Positif*, n° 110, November 1969.

SYLVIE PIERRE, "Il était une fois dans l'Ouest." *Cahiers du Cinéma*, n° 218, March 1970.

ANDREW SARRIS, "Once Upon a Time in the West." *The Village Voice*, 6 August 1970.

SANDRO GRAZIANI, "Western italiano-western americano." *Bianco e Nero*, n°ˢ 9-10, September-October 1970.

PIERRE LACHAT, "Der Italo-Western." *Cinema* (Adliswil, Switzerland), n° 61, 1970.

STEFAN MORAWSKI, "Spaghetti Western Wedtug Leone." *Kino*, n° 6, 1970, Warsaw.

MIKE WALLINGTON, "Italian Westerns - A Concordance." *Cinema*, n°ˢ 6-7, August 1970, Cambridge.

CHRIS FRAYLING, "Sergio Leone." *Cinema* n°ˢ 6-7, August 1970, Cambridge.

PIERRE BAUDRY, "L'idéologie du western italien." *Cahiers du cinéma*, n° 233, November 1971.

GASTON HAUSTRATE, "Faut-il brûler les westerns italiens?" *Cinéma 71*, n° 154, March 1971.

GUY BRAUCOURT, "Il était une fois la Révolution." *Ecran 72*, n° 5, May 1972.

MANUEL DORI, "Sergio Leone" in *Il western*, edited by Raymond Bellour, Feltrinelli, Milan, 1973.

LJUBOMIR OLIVA, "Western krizem krázem." *Film a doba*, n° 7, 1973.

NOËL SIMSOLO, "Notes sur les westerns de Sergio Leone." *La revue de cinéma*, n° 275, September 1973.

RICHARD JAMESON, "A Fistful of Sergio Leone." *Film Comment*, March-April 1973 and March-April 1974.

STUART KAMINSKY, "The Grotesque West of Sergio Leone." *Take One*, May 1973.

STUART KAMINSKY, "The Italian Western Beyond Leone." *The Velvet Light Trap*, n° 12, 1974.

EDUARDO GEODA, "Mitologia e iconografia del western-spaghetti." *Cinefilo*, n° 25, 1974.

VITTORIO SPINAZZOLA, "Cinema e pubblico (Lo spettacolo filmico in Italia 1945-1965)." Bompiani, Milan, 1974.

LINO MICCICHÉ, "Il cinema italiano degli anni '60." Marsilio, Venice, 1975.

CLAUDINE EIZYKMAN, "La jouissance-cinéma." Union Générale d'Editions, Paris, 1976.

IGNACIO RAMONET, "Westerns italiens – Cinéma politique." *Le Monde diplomatique*, October 1976.

GIAN PIERO BRUNETTA, "Storia del cinema italiano (Dal 1945 agli anni ottanta)." Editori Riuniti, Rome, 1982.

GIUSEPPE RAUSA, "Interni rapporti di complicità tra western e melodramma in Sergio Leone." *Segno Cinema*, n° 13, May-June 1984.

MARY CORLISS, "Once Upon a Time in America." *Film Comment*, 1984.

PIERA DETASSIS, "C'era una volta in America." *Bianco e Nero*, n° 4, 1984.

EMANUELA MARTINI, "C'era una volta in America." *Cineforum*, n° 238, October 1984.

JOSÉ MARIA LATORRE, "Hasta que llegó su hora." *Dirigido por...*, n° 133, February 1986.

CLAVER SALIZZATO (Ed.), "Il cinema di Sergio Leone." *Cinecritica*, n°s 11-12, October 1988-March 1989.

BILL KROHN, "La planète Leone." *Cahiers du cinéma*, n° 422, July-August 1989.

VINCENT OSTRIA, "Il était une fois dans l'Ouest." *Cahiers du cinéma*, special issue 1993: *100 films pour une vidéothèque*.

SERGE TOUBIANA, "Il était une fois en Amérique." *Cahiers du cinéma*, special issue 1993: *100 films pour une vidéothèque*.

MARCELLO GAROFALO (Ed.), "Il cinema-Leone" (Writings by Garofalo, Silvestri, Fittante, Giusti, Caprara, Avondola, Pugliese, Canova, Crespi, Morandini, Ghezzi), *Segno Cinema*, n° 67, May-June 1994 and n° 68, July-August 1994.

Principal interviews with Sergio Leone:

In addition to the interviews contained in the books of Franco Ferreri, Gilles Lambert, Massimo Moscati, Nöel Simsolo, Francesco Minnini, Roberto Lasagna, and in the book *Per un pugno di dollari* (edited by Luca Verdone), also deserving mention are the interviews made by Guy Braucourt in *Cinéma 69* n° 140, November 1969, and in *Ecran 72*, May 1972 and by Angelo Lucano in *La rivista del cinematografico*, January 1967, and by Roberto Pugliese in *Segno Cinema* n° 12, March 1984.

Screenplays:

Per un pugno di dollari (A Fistful of Dollars): complete shooting script after final editing and original dialogues, by Luca Verdone, Cappelli, Bologna, 1979.

C'era una volta il West (Once Upon a Time in the Ouest): only the complete shooting script of the final showdown after final editing, and the original shooting script of scenes cut in the Italian commercial version; Franco Ferrini *L'antiwestern e il caso Leone, Bianco e Nero*, Rome, 1971.

Giù la testa (Duck! You Sucker): complete shooting script after final editing, and original dialogues, in Franco Ferrini, op. cit.

C'era una volta in America (Once Upon a Time in America): only the complete shooting script of scenes cut in the Italian release version; *Il cinema di Sergio Leone*, cit., edited by Claver Salizzato.

C'era una volta in America (Once Upon a Time in America): only the scenes cut in the Italian commercial version; *Il cinema di Sergio Leone*, cit., edited by Claver Salizzato.

Writings by Sergio Leone:

Introduction to J. Hembus, *Western Lexicon*, Hanser-Verlag, Munich, 1976.

"A John Ford, un suo allievo: dal West con amore." *Corriere della Sera*, August 20, 1983.

Preface to Harry Grey, *Mano armata*, Longanesi, Milan, 1983.

Preface to Diego Gabutti, *C'era una volta in America*, cit.

"Per i novant'anni del cinema." *L'Unità*, December 28, 1985.

"Per il decimo anniversario della morte di Chaplin." *L'Unità*, December 26, 1987.

Introduction to Gianni Di Claudio, *Il cinema western*, Libreria Universitaria Editrice, Chieti, 1986.

Introduction to Marcello Garofalo, *C'era una volta in America (Photographic Memories)*, cit.

"Venivamo da ogni parte del mondo." *Bianco e Nero*, n° 4, October-December 1988.

Films and videos on Sergio Leone:

TOMMASO CHIARETTI, MARIO MORINI, *Western primo amore*, presented by Franco Parenti (Sergio Leone comments the mythology of the Western), RAI RADIOTELEVISIONE ITALIANA, 1974.

GIANNI MINÀ, *C'era una volta il cinema. Sergio Leone e i suoi film*, RAI, 1985.

LUCA VERDONE, *Sergio Leone*, Presidenza del Consiglio dei Ministri, Dipartimento Editoria, 1996.

CLAVER SALIZZATO, *Sentieri selvaggi. Scene segrete di Sergio Leone*, Sergio Leone Production, 1996.